BEETHOVEN'S COMPOSITIONAL CHOICES

STUDIES IN THE CRITICISM AND THEORY OF MUSIC

General Editor
Leonard B. Meyer

Editorial Board
Monroe C. Beardsley
Edward T. Cone
Janet M. Levy
Robert P. Morgan
Eugene Narmour

BEETHOVEN'S COMPOSITIONAL CHOICES

The Two Versions of Opus 18, No. 1, First Movement

JANET M. LEVY

UNIVERSITY OF PENNSYLVANIA PRESS
PHILADELPHIA · 1982

The musical examples for both versions of Beethoven's Opus 18, No. 1, First Movement are based on the Beethoven *Werke* edition and are used with permission of G. Henle Verlag.

Library of Congress Cataloging in Publication Data
Levy, Janet M.
    Beethoven's compositional choices.
    (Studies in the criticism and theory of music)
    1. Beethoven, Ludwig van, 1770–1828. Quartets, strings, no. 1, op. 18,
no. 1, F major. Allegro con brio. 2. Music—Analysis, appreciation.
I. Title. II. Series.
ML410.B4L5345 1982   785.7'0092'4   82-60300
ISBN 0-8122-7850-X

Printed in the United States of America

For my mother and father

CONTENTS

ACKNOWLEDGMENTS

Since this study was first completed in 1977 it has, perhaps under the influence of the object of its study, existed in several versions. And, like the object of its study, it is often small changes—matters of detail—that seem significantly to have improved it. In revising the manuscript I have benefited from the heterogeneously helpful comments of a number of colleagues and friends: Wye Allanbrook, Bathia Churgin, Barbara Hanning, David Lidov, Eugene Narmour, Ellen Rosand, Ruth Solie, and Peter Gram Swing. I am especially indebted to Joseph Kerman for his careful and responsive reading of several versions of the manuscript and for his many valuable suggestions, and to William Thomson for detailed and provocative criticism. For their generous words of encouragement I am grateful to Lawrence Bernstein, Wallace Berry, and, particularly, Richard Swift.

Long before this essay was begun, my teacher, Leonard G. Ratner, had already stirred my interest in the Beethoven quartets. My analytic point of view owes an incalculable debt to all my study with him. Early in my work on the two versions of Op. 18, No. 1, the former Hampshire Quartet—Lucy Bardo, Genette Foster, Joan Kalisch, Dorothy Strahl—graciously read through and allowed me to record its reading of the first version of the quartet. My thanks to each.

Finally, the most traditional acknowledgment—to one's spouse—cannot in any way be construed traditionally. For not only has my husband listened endlessly and patiently to my ideas and endured life through several versions of the manuscript, but he has sympathetically read and responded to every page—some several times over. Above all, our dialogues and debates have profoundly affected my thinking about music.

PREFACE

THIS VOLUME IS THE FIRST in a series of books and monographs, "Studies in the Criticism and Theory of Music," to be published by the University of Pennsylvania Press. It seems appropriate, therefore, that the general editor write a preface defining the rationale of the series, its orientation and its goals, and the kinds of scholarly studies to be published. Doing so, however, would probably not be prudent. Paradoxically, the circumstances that make the inauguration of the series important are precisely those that make writing such a preface problematic.

Music theory seems presently to be in something akin to what Thomas S. Kuhn has called a preparadigm period*—a period in which discussion tends to deteriorate into sometimes acrimonious and often unproductive debate about first principles. The heady temptation of philosophical dispute impedes inquiry by dividing scholars into cliques and claques, and the controversies thus engendered tend to divert energies from current, pressing intellectual concerns. These involve building bit by bit, through exemplary individual studies, a repertory of scrupulous criticism and a corpus of coherent theoretical concepts. Not only would the doubts and demurrals occasioned by a disquisition delving into "fundamentals"—for instance, the differences between criticism and analysis, the nature of music theory, the proper role of quantification, the relevance of related disciplines such as psychology or linguistics—draw attention away from the task of *doing* (as opposed to talking "about") criticism and theory, but an adequate discussion of the issues involved would require a separate and extensive essay.

It can scarcely be controversial, however, to observe that criticism and theory are complementary disciplines. For criticism can illuminate and evaluate the relationships peculiar to particular compositions only if it is grounded upon general principles of some sort—upon theory, however informal. Conversely, the peculiar relationships that define the structure and process of individual compositions constitute the indispensable basis for the formulation of a theory of music. This interdependency suggests another: namely, both criticism and theory seek to understand and explain the choices made by composers. Criticism is concerned to account for the choices made in specific compositions, while

The Structure of Scientific Revolutions (Chicago, 1962), p. 47f.

theory is concerned to discover the general nature of, and the relationships among, the cognitive, stylistic, and cultural constraints that govern compositional choice.

From this point of view, it would be difficult to find a more fitting way to inaugurate "Studies in the Criticism and Theory of Music" than with a monograph that, without either the paraphernalia of abstruse language or the protective shield of systematic doctrine, explicitly undertakes the complex, intriguing, and in this case inescapable task of accounting for the specific choices made by a particular composer.

Leonard B. Meyer, General Editor
University of Pennsylvania

1

THE NATURE OF THE PROBLEM

IT IS WELL KNOWN that two complete versions of Beethoven's String Quartet Op. 18, No. 1 exist. The version of the quartet that everyone knows as Op. 18, No. 1 is indeed the one Beethoven considered and published as such. This is the second complete version of the quartet, published by Mollo in 1801.[1] The first version, itself a complete work, exists as a set of manuscript parts in a copyist's hand[2] and was inscribed by Beethoven on June 25, 1799 as a gift for his friend, the violinist Karl Amenda: "Dear Amenda: Take this quartet as a small memorial of our friendship, and whenever you play it recall the days which we passed together and the sincere affection felt for you then and which will always be felt by / Your warm and true friend / Ludwig van Beethoven."[3] Perhaps what is best known about this version is the often-quoted remark Beethoven made when he wrote Amenda on July 1, 1801 and asked him not to circulate the copy he gave him: "Do not lend your quartet to anybody, because I have greatly changed it, having just learned how to write quartets properly."[4] What did Beethoven mean?

1. Likely in June 1801. On the basis of Beethoven's correspondence, it appears that the first three quartets of Op. 18 were sent to the publisher in the autumn of 1800. See *Thayer's Life of Beethoven*, ed. Elliot Forbes, rev. ed. (Princeton, 1967), pp. 260–61, 264. The autographs of the Op. 18 quartets have disappeared.

2. Since 1913 in the archives of the Beethovenhaus, Bonn. (There is a microfilm copy of this set of parts in the Toscanini Archives at the New York Public Library.) The development section of the first movement seems to have been the first part of the original quartet to appear in print, as a supplement of music entitled "Durchführung des Ersten Satzes von Beethovens F-Dur Streichquartett Op. 18 No. 1 in der Gegenüberstellung beider Fassungen," in Carl Waack, "Beethovens F-dur Streichquartett Op. 18 No. 1 in seiner ursprünglichen Fassung," *Die Musik* 3, no. 12 (1904): 418–20. The entire first version appeared as a supplement in Hans Josef Wedig, "Beethovens Streichquartett op. 18 nr. 1 und seine erste Fassung," *Veröffentlichungen des Beethovenhauses in Bonn*, vol. 2 (Bonn, 1922). All four movements (first version) were published by Willy Hess in the *Supplemente zur Gesamtausgabe*, vol. 6 (Wiesbaden, 1963); and in the new Beethoven *Werke*, ser. 6, vol. 3 (Streichquartette I), ed. Paul Mies (Munich, 1962).

For a discussion of the copyist for the first movement (probably Schlemmer), see Alan Tyson, "Notes on Five of Beethoven's Copyists," *Journal of the American Musicological Society* 23 (1970): 443–46.

3. The inscription is on the title page of the first violin part (marked "Quartetto Nr. II") and is reproduced in facsimile in the frontispiece of the new Beethoven *Werke*, ser. 6, vol. 3. This translation comes from *Thayer's Life of Beethoven*, p. 224.

Karl Friedrich Amenda (1771–1836) was a teacher in the service of Prince Lobkowitz (to whom the second version of the quartet is dedicated) and apparently an intimate friend of Beethoven. Details of the relationship between Amenda and Beethoven can be found in most standard sources on Beethoven. See especially *Thayer's Life of Beethoven*, pp. 223–25.

4. *Thayer's Life of Beethoven*, p. 262. The complete letter is given in *The Letters of Beethoven*, ed. and trans. Emily Anderson (London, 1961), vol. 1, p. 65 (Letter 53). The original German text may be found in Waack, "Beethovens F-dur Streichquartett." According to Sieghard Brandenburg, the autograph letter is in Bonn, Beethovenhaus, Bodmer collection, BBr 1 ("The First Version of Beethoven's G Major String Quartet, Op. 18 No. 2," *Music and Letters* 58 [1977]: 127).

Despite the fact that the existence of the first version of the quartet has been known since the late nineteenth century,[5] only a few scholars have sought to suggest what Beethoven might have meant when he wrote Amenda that he had "just learned how to write quartets properly." Since the publication of the development section of the first movement by Carl Waack in 1904,[6] the possibility of careful inquiry has been before us. Waack himself commented only generally on the greater concision and concentration in the whole second version and on a few matters of detail in the development section of the first movement (for example, the heightened preparation for the recapitulation); he also observed that the expressive character was essentially the same in both versions. In his 1922 study, Wedig, like Waack, was struck by the overall compression in the opening movement of the second version and especially by the revisions in the development.[7] For Wedig the latter revisions were the only truly important ones because he viewed changes such as those in voice-leading, instrumentation, dynamics, and the like as significant primarily for what they might reveal about Beethoven's workshop, not for their intrinsic importance to the syntax of the movement. His point of view was in many ways a very nineteenth-century one: most of the revisions were interpreted or "explained" in terms of their immediate expressive effects and not in terms of formal and syntactic relationships. For example, revised dynamics or accompaniments were "explained" simply on the basis of their being "more urgent" or "more peaceful."[8] In more recent general studies of Beethoven's quartets, there has been no sustained address to the question of how we might understand Beethoven's remarks.[9]

The task of understanding Beethoven's compositional choices for the second, the published version, as compared with those in the first, is different from that of most existing studies of his compositional practice. It does not lie in the realm of history. For instance, the impulse for a second version cannot be traced to external reasons, as it can with the String Quintet Op. 104, the Leonore Overtures, and the oratorio *Christus am Oelberge*.[10] And, except in the most general sense, the changes Beethoven made cannot be traced to or explained by his contrapuntal studies or his relationships with patron princes at the time. Further, since the autographs are lost, one does not have a task of disentangling versions through layers of corrections, as with the autograph of the Sonata for Violoncello and Piano, Op. 69.[11] Nor is it a case of sketches in relation to a completed work. As it happens, only a

5. Primarily through Ludwig Nohl. See Brandenburg, "The First Version of Op. 18 No. 2," p. 127.

6. Waack, "Beethovens F-dur Streichquartett."

7. Wedig, "Beethovens Streichquartett Op. 18, nr. 1."

8. Ibid., pp. 18 and 22.

9. For example, Joseph Kerman, *The Beethoven Quartets* (New York, 1967), pp. 31–34; and Daniel Gregory Mason, *The Quartets of Beethoven* (New York, 1947), pp. 21–23.

10. Alan Tyson discusses each of these multiversion (two or more) works in three articles: "The Authors of the Op. 104 String Quintet," in *Beethoven Studies*, ed. Alan Tyson (New York, 1973), pp. 158–73; "The Problems of Beethoven's 'First' Leonore Overture," *Journal of the American Musicological Society* 28 (1975): 292–334; "The 1803 Version of Beethoven's *Christus am Oelberge*," in *The Creative World of Beethoven*, ed. Paul Henry Lang (New York, 1971), pp. 49–82. In the case of the Op. 104 String Quintet, an arrangement of the C Minor Piano Trio, Op. 1, No. 3, "the external stimulus . . . was Beethoven's dissatisfaction with an arrangement that had been completed by someone else" (p. 158). In general, the Leonore Overtures—their plurality, as Tyson puts it—may be linked to various productions of the opera itself, or at least to the prospect of a production (in Prague, for the Leonore Overture No. 1). The matter of external impulses for *Christus am Oelberge* is less clear-cut, but surely related to Beethoven's problems with the text, various textual revisions, and possibly the critical reception of the oratorio.

11. See Lewis Lockwood, "The Autograph of the First Movement of Beethoven's Sonata for Violoncello and Pianoforte, Opus 69," in *The Music Forum*, vol. 2, ed. William J. Mitchell and Felix Salzer (New York, 1970), pp. 1–109. Both here, and in his article, "On Beethoven's Sketches and Autographs: Some Problems of Definition and Interpretation," *Acta Musicologica* 42 (1970): 32–47, Lockwood discusses the different phases of realization found in different sections of the first movement of the Op. 69 Sonata; he points out that "one can unravel two full-length versions of the entire development section, of which the second version . . . represents a total recasting and exchange of the roles of the Violoncello and Piano" (quote from the *Acta* article, p. 38).

few short sketches for the first movement are unequivocally attributable to the revision, the second version.[12] Consequently, one is not grappling with the order of revisions—whether, for example, Beethoven changed one section before another or revised melodic relationships before rhythmic ones. The present essay, then, is not about the progress of Beethoven's thought as evidenced in stages from sketches to final version; it is not a study of his style of working.[13]

Indeed, even were a sketch study of the revision (from first to second version) possible, it would be essentially different from the one embarked upon here. The nature of the difference is a complex and subtle one. It involves questions of the sort that we ask when we try to determine when a human being is a human being and no longer an embryo. Is it a difference merely in degree or is it a difference in kind? To address such issues properly would require another essay, but a few points are germane here.

A very simple observation may help to illuminate the nature of the difference. A complete version of a work, such as the first version of Op. 18, No. 1 can be performed.[14] It makes sense on its own as a work of art and can exist by itself (like a human being and unlike an embryo), so to speak, out in the world. The sketches cannot—not, at least, in the same sense. This difference suggests a fundamental difference in kind between sketch-to-work analysis and a study of two versions of one work. Just as a complete first version can be performed, it can also, unlike the sketches, be interpreted by a critic. Its internal relationships are known. The analyst-critic can discuss how well a passage or structural moment is realized, how certain features might be improved, and so forth, just as he can for the version Beethoven allowed to stand. For, with a complete version of a work, the "goals" (broadly interpreted, the cardinal structural and expressive characteristics) are knowable in a way that they are not with the sketches. But we cannot assume that the goals of a completed work are necessarily the same as the goals of the sketches for it. Conceivably, the composer might have made some sketches in connection with goals other than those he ultimately settled on. That is, one cannot ascertain whether sketch X was made with goal Y (as apprehended in the finished work) in mind, or with some other, even unknown goal—perhaps one not even hinted at in the extant sketches *or* the work. Indeed, patent similarity or even identity between a sketch and part of the final work does not deny the validity of this point. The composer may have understood and revised his "goals" only *after* sketching. (All of us will recognize that we often discover or redefine our goals in the very process of writing.)

Here, however, are two complete versions of the "same" work. The first, or Amenda, version, with its parts copied out by a copyist, must have been considered a completed work

12. These are in Landsberg 7, p. 1, staffs 3–4 and 5–8. A transcription of this sketch manuscript is given in Karl Lothar Mikulicz, *Ein Notierungsbuch von Beethoven aus dem Besitz der Preussischen Staatsbibliothek zu Berlin* (Leipzig, 1927; reprint ed., Hildesheim, 1972), p. 1.

There are a considerable number of sketches for the *first*, the 1799 version of the first movement. These are primarily in Grasnick 1 and 2. For Grasnick 2, see Wilhelm Virneisel, *Beethoven: Ein Skizzenbuch zu Streichquartetten aus op. 18* (Bonn, 1974). Detailed accounts of sketch location and chronology for the Op. 18 quartets are found in Richard Kramer, "The Sketches for Beethoven's Violin Sonata, Opus 30" (Ph.D. diss., Princeton University, 1974), vol. 1, especially chap. 5 and pp. 134–37; also see Brandenburg, "The First Version of Op. 18 No. 2," pp. 127–52.

13. For example, to learn that, for a particular passage in the retransition of the first movement of his Sixth Symphony, Beethoven sketched out "two versions, side by side . . . as if to weigh their relative advantages" (Philip Gossett, "Beethoven's Sixth Symphony: Sketches for the First Movement," *Journal of the American Musicological Society* 27 [1974]: 259). For provocative general discussions of the nature of sketch studies, see John M. Ellis, *The Theory of Literary Criticism: A Logical Analysis* (Berkeley, 1974), chap. 5, especially pp. 114–23; and Douglas Johnson, "Beethoven Scholars and Beethoven's Sketches," *19th-Century Music* 2 (1978): 3–17 (especially p. 13ff.).

14. Indeed, the Pro Arte Quartet recently recorded the complete original version of Op. 18, No. 1. The recording was issued (1981) on Laurel Record, LR–116.

THE NATURE OF THE PROBLEM 3

of art by Beethoven at the time he gave it to Amenda. Only later did Beethoven apparently regard this version as a somewhat botched draft.[15] The second version always had the status of a "work of art." In both versions all events are *in place*, the total internal context fixed, all the relationships fully given. This allows for a kind of analytic-critical control that is not often possible in Beethoven studies. Precisely because, in a broad sense, there are few revisions of basic structural relationships, because the major goals are clear, and because the decisive points in the large form are essentially constant, we can look especially closely at what Beethoven was about, at his strategies for improving the realization of fundamentally the same goals. The two complete versions of the quartet challenge us directly. A new kind of comparison is called for.

To understand why Beethoven considered the second version an improvement, it is not enough to describe the revisions; what is required is an attempt to explain as precisely as possible what the revisions accomplished.[16] In doing so, one is continually forced back to first questions about the nature of relationships in tonal music, and thus to theory. But there is no single systematic theory that can adequately explain the revisions Beethoven made. Thus, though I hope that my own viewpoint is consistent, it does not espouse or adhere to any single theoretical or analytical framework, old or new, of others or my own.[17] Although all the movements of the quartet were revised, the first movement, if taken by itself, is an abundant source of exemplary material for a study of the nature of Beethoven's compositional choices. And an analysis of Beethoven's revisions as they exemplify compositional problems and solutions is the primary concern of this essay.

Most of the changes that Beethoven made affect formal clarity and the direction of movement. Broadly speaking, they relate to articulation, to continuity and mobility, and to coherence. If there is disagreement about the explanation for a given change, there is less likely to be disagreement about its general effect—for example, that a given change either promotes or weakens closure, increases or reduces ambiguity. This kind of study makes evident something that anyone who has grappled with problems in analysis knows: from moment to moment in a composition the various parameters exert different degrees of influence in defining structural functions and character. Thus, although several or all parameters will probably be involved in any single change Beethoven makes, there will be occasions when the discussion will focus only on those that seem to be most significant in effecting the change. Similarly, both large-scale structure and local syntax are likely to be involved in *each* change, but sometimes I shall deal with the immediate and not the long-range effect of a revision, and at other times vice versa.

A number of Beethoven's changes, such as those in part-writing, do not substantially

15. On the basis of his investigation of sketches, Brandenburg posits that there once existed a complete first version of Op. 18, No. 2, radically different from the known published version; see Brandenburg, "The First Version of Op. 18 No. 2," pp. 127–52, especially pp. 143 and 152.

16. To be sure, we do not know how Beethoven might have explained his changes. And we do not literally know what he "wanted" or "intended." But we can consider how the changes "work" and why they make sense, given our knowledge of the style and the state of our theoretical knowledge.

In my attempt to account for what Beethoven's revisions accomplished, it may at times seem from my analysis that there is no question but that all Beethoven's changes improve the final version. Although my explanations of certain changes may be viable, other considerations may lead some of us still to prefer passages in the first version. That is, a particular change may be understood as an improvement in significant respects, but it does not follow that the overall effect will necessarily be more pleasing. I know at least two sensitive musicians who regret that Beethoven removed one eight-measure passage! This, in spite of the fact that both understand the way in which the removal of the passage tightened the structure.

17. The meanings of the analytic vocabulary will, I hope, be clear from its use and its context. There are no "code words": words and phrases such as "mobility," "local syntax," and "telescoping," as well as "process" and "ambiguity," are to be understood essentially as they are in ordinary language.

affect the organization of the movement, but they serve to clarify local syntax. Paradoxically, such clarifications may entail an increase in the ambiguity of a passage, where ambiguity *is* the syntactic goal. In other cases a revision not merely clarifies or intensifies an existing function, but also alters that function; that is, a revision may change syntax, be it that of a complete musical period or a short musical unit such as a motive.

In a manner reminiscent of commentaries on the first movement of Beethoven's Fifth Symphony, critics of the first movement of Op. 18, No. 1 (final version) have made much of its saturation with the initial turn motive. Indeed, "motivic exhaustion" ("using up" a motive by employing it in every conceivable way) has been viewed, at least implicitly, as an aspect of Beethoven's progress as a composer and has been a favorite topic in discussions of this movement. In the light of this preoccupation with motivic saturation—a preoccupation that seems to reflect the influence of the biological model—it is particularly interesting to note that in his revision Beethoven actually *removed* many occurrences of the turn motive.[18] Further, in this connection it is intriguing that the majority of deletions of the motive can be interpreted as a means of tightening the structure!

The large-scale structural plan of the movement is essentially not the province of this essay. It was set, both by tradition and by Beethoven. This is clearly indicated by the fact that the very beginnings of the exposition, development, recapitulation, and coda, as well as the very ends of the same segments, are, with one exception, basically the same in both versions. The exception, the end of the development, is telling; it emphasizes that the parts of the form that are traditionally most processive (parts such as the retransition and the transitions between key areas) are generally the most changed. Even though, broadly speaking, process is changed, certain features of process are constant, such as the presence of a fugato in both developments and a build to a forceful recapitulation in both versions. (The internal nature of these passages *is* revised.) And though large form is essentially constant, the fact that Beethoven removed the repeat sign and the first ending of the recapitulation is obviously a significant change in large proportions and length.[19]

As the most substantively revised segment of the movement, the development is especially revealing. However, many of the changes in the exposition, recapitulation, and coda claim attention not only for their importance to the movement, but as examples of Beethoven's compositional concerns.[20] Despite its length and amount of detail, my essay does not attempt to consider all the changes Beethoven made; nor does it presume to account fully for those that are considered. An explanation of the changes requires continual comparison of one version with the other, and for this reason the essay will proceed seriatim—beginning with the opening of the exposition.

18. Kerman tallied no fewer than 130 occurrences of the turn motive in the first version and only 104 occurrences in the second version (*Beethoven Quartets*, p. 32).

Interestingly, Wedig, whose own thinking tends to reflect nineteenth-century attitudes, caught A. B. Marx (?1795–1866) on this very subject! Wedig took a wry view of Marx's remark that the first movement of Op. 18, No. 1 is more "Beethovenian" than the first movement of the D major Quartet, Op. 18, No. 3, largely because of its "quartetlike" exhaustion of the single "head-motive." With his knowledge of Version 1 (which presumably Marx did not have), Wedig could point out that if such motivic exhaustion were the measure of the work, Version 1 would take first prize, for it has more occurrences of the head-motive than Version 2; see Wedig, "Beethovens Streichquartett Op. 18, nr. 1," p. 17.

19. Among the first movements of Op. 18, only Nos. 5 and 6 call for a reprise of part 2 (i.e., the development-plus recapitulation). Even with the repeat of part 2 (together with that of part 1) neither of these movements is as long as the first movement of Op. 18, No. 1 in its original version, with both repeats taken. (The Pro Arte Quartet's recording [see n. 14] lasts nearly fourteen minutes, considerably longer than most performances of the first movement of Beethoven's Eighth Symphony with the exposition repeated.) The repeat of the development-plus-recapitulation was becoming an archaic feature and perhaps Beethoven merely carried it over in a routine way.

20. One is speaking, of course, about inferences made on the basis of Beethoven's revisions.

2

EXPOSITION

KEY AREA I
(Measures 1–29)

ALTHOUGH THE PRINCIPAL REVISIONS in the exposition occur in the transition and the second key area, one change in the first key area—the very first in the piece—seems more significant than others.[21] It is the addition, in measure 5, Version 2,[22] of second violin, viola, and cello, and the presentation of IV^6 harmony (Ex. 1).[23] This change from an unspecified and somewhat ambiguous harmony (which might be heard as I or VI, as well as IV) to an explicit IV^6 chord, helps to make clear that the form of the opening eight measures is 2 + 2 + 4 measures. The specification of the harmony in Version 2 binds measure 5 more closely with the following three measures; the succession of first-inversion harmonies enhances goal-directed motion toward the half-cadence at measure 8 and, in turn, toward the strong harmonic closure that follows the half-cadence. Moreover, as the first deviation from the unison sound of the opening four measures, the new texture combines with the spelling out of the harmony to signal the grouping of this measure with its successive rather than with immediately preceding measures. (In both versions, measure 5 groups with measures 6–8 but it does so more clearly in Version 2.)

Importantly, by making this change, Beethoven functionally differentiates measure 5 from measure 13 (which is the same in both versions). As a result, the solo treatment of measure 13 in Version 2 is more clearly a sign of the beginning of a new pattern of action (different from that which follows measure 5), a sequence from measures 13 to 20. Finally, in Version 2, the added voices in measure 5 help to effect the ⟍ ⟋ Beethoven now calls for between measures 5 and 6. The ⟍ ⟋ not only further differentiates measure 5 from measure 13 in Version 2 but, by differentiating measure 5 from measure 1, it also emphasizes the more integrated rhythmic structure of the opening: 2 + 2 + 4 measures. This was implicit in Version 1, but there the organization might be regarded as an additive 2 + 2 + 2 + 2 or 2 + 2 + 1 + 3. Thus, the seemingly small revisions of one measure (m. 5) significantly affect the clarity of the initial statement of the movement.

21. The other revisions of the first key area are primarily in register (single-octave transpositions) and dynamics; there are several small rhythmic changes as well (m. 8, viola; m. 18, cello; m. 26, viola and cello; m. 27, cello). Needless to say, even a single registral or dynamic change can be highly important to the structure and process of a movement; this will be evident, for example, in the discussion of the second key area. But the registral and dynamic changes in the first key area do not seem as significant as most of the subsequent changes in the movement.

22. Throughout this study Version 2 refers to the revised version, the one authorized for publication by Beethoven, the

Example 1

one that has come down to us as *the* Op. 18, No. 1 String Quartet.

23. The examples are based on the Mies edition of both versions in the new *Werke*. See n. 2 above.

Beethoven's revisions of the transition serve, above all, to underline the syntax that is characteristic of transitions. For purposes of discussion, this section will be divided: measures 30–37, beginning; measures 37–55, second part (mm. 37–41, 41–49, 49–55).

Measures 30–37

Revisions of inner parts soften punctuation and division.

Though relatively small in themselves, Beethoven's revisions in measures 30–37 (Ex. 2) help to make it clear that the transition, the period of motion away from the home key, is beginning.[24] In both versions Beethoven starts to undermine the stability of the first key almost immediately after its emphatic confirmation on the first beat of measure 29.[25] After just one beat of tonic in root position, the $\frac{6}{3}$ position of the harmony (beats 2 and 3, m. 29) suggests a weakening of the stability of F major; and the $\frac{6}{4}$ position of the tonic in measure 30 of both versions increases harmonic instability. All of Beethoven's revisions in the ensuing measures (mm. 30–37) further weaken the stability of key and rhythmic structure. Generally, these changes result in a *less* decisive phrase structure in Version 2 and, in turn, a more cohesive and unitary motion away from the home key.

In Version 1, the viola's skips of G–B♭ and A–C on the first beats of measures *31* and *33*, as well as the two-measure alternations of the predominant pitch—from C (mm. *29–30*) to B♭ (mm. *31–32*) and back to C (mm. *33–34*)—produce a clear 2 + 2 grouping of measures in the inner parts.[26] Action in the second violin joins with that of the viola: the change from a single note to a double-stop within the first beats of measures *29*, *31*, and *33* emphasizes articulation every two measures in the inner parts. Strong and weak measures in the first violin part are the same as those of the inner parts,[27] namely: m. *29 30 31 32 33 34*. Thus, because of identical accents, the three upper parts tend to dominate the rhythm on the measure-to-measure level (Ex. 2a).

In *this* context, the cello part tends to be heard as congruent with the upper parts: ♩ ♫♫|♩ . That is, the upper parts seem to assimilate the intrinsic beginning-accented pattern of the cello motive (♩ ♫♫|♩) as it is understood from its initial presentation in the very first measure of the movement.[28] Despite the fact that initially (even in this context) the cello motive in Version 1 is likely to be heard as beginning-accented, our sense of its accent pattern is immediately revised in measure *31* where the upper three parts have "prior claim," partly because their patterning was begun first (m. *29*, in the inner parts), and then

---

24. This period is not completed until the cadence at measure 72.

25. As Leonard G. Ratner writes of this movement in "Key Definition—A Structural Issue in Beethoven's Music," *Journal of the American Musicological Society* 23 (1970): 476, "The home key is defined in four increasingly strong gestures: (1) as a unison in measure 1; (2) in the half-cadence of measure 8; (3) in a rather light authentic cadence at measure 20; and (4) in a broadly emphatic cadence at measure 29."

26. For the sake of clarity, the measure numbers for Version 1 will be italicized.

27. The signs — and ‿ are used to symbolize strong and weak pulses, beats, measures, etc., respectively; in a more general way, they indicate relative stability and instability, respectively, on whatever level is being symbolized. Brackets indicate groupings of stable and unstable events. This type of prosodic symbolization is used not only by such contemporary theorists as Grosvenor W. Cooper and Leonard B. Meyer in *The Rhythmic Structure of Music* (Chicago, 1960), Edward T. Cone in *Musical Form and Musical Performance* (New York, 1968), and Wallace Berry in *Structural Functions in Music* (Englewood Cliffs, 1976), but also by a number of eighteenth-century theorists, among them Heinrich Christoph Koch and Johannes Mattheson.

(See pp. 10, 11 for notes 28–30.)

---

reinforced by the first violin's patterning (m. *30*, upbeat; m. *31*, downbeat). In addition, the second measure of the turn motive in the cello is played on the open C string; and, again in *this* context, the natural stress of the open string, combined with the other factors, makes the end of the cello pattern (mm. *31*, *33*, *35*) seem accented.

Beethoven's changes in measures 30–37 suggest that he regarded the passage in Version 1 as overly punctuated.[29] At measures 31 and 33 in Version 2, he removes the articulation on the first beat in the viola and softens that in the second violin; he also maintains the tone C in the viola in eighth-note motion between measures 29 and 35, as a kind of ground—uniform and unobtrusive. These changes in the inner parts serve to deemphasize division into two-measure units (as compared with mm. *31*, *33*, *35* of Version 1). Although the harmony at measure 32 is essentially dominant seventh in both versions, in Version 2 the absence of the pronounced seventh (as in mm. *31–32* of Version 1) and its resolution (to A, m. *33*) in the viola combines with the changed position of the chord to reduce considerably the separation of phrase from phrase.

A result of the weakened articulation of the inner parts in Version 2 is that, if properly performed, the cello's turn motive can be heard throughout the passage with its own original accent pattern, that is, as beginning-accented. This patterning conflicts with that in the first violin (Ex. 2b). The overlapping of patterns at once bonds the whole passage more closely and makes it more unstable than it was in Version 1. In both versions the passage is mobile. But in Version 1 mobility springs from an almost blatant regularity, in Version 2 from subtle syntactic ambiguity.

Example 2

Rhythmic ambiguity enhances mobility as motion away from the home key begins.

As the transition continues (Ex. 3, m. 37ff.), other changes, again matters of small detail, continue to enhance the syntax characteristic of transitions. In both versions the transitional character is unmistakable at measure 37ff. because it is there that the first clear harmonic motion away from the orbit of F major occurs and because the harmonic rhythm accelerates (one change per measure rather than every two). But in Version 2 the syntax is markedly clearer.

In Version 1 the sforzandi foster the continuation of a marchlike regularity of two-measure groupings; in short, a basically undisturbed regularity governs its rhythmic structure (m. *29ff.*). Although the harmony at measure 37 is anacrustic in both versions— V/VI (m. 37) moving to VI (m. 38)—in Version 1 the sforzandi in all parts coordinate with the "on-schedule" change in harmony from measure 36 to continue the patterning of strong to weak measures begun at measure 29 (m. 29, strong; m. 30, weak, etc.). Moreover, in Version 1 the sforzando combines with the tie of the ♩ in the first violin part (mm. *37–38*) to the next measure (m. *38*) to negate, or at least considerably weaken, the upbeat aspect of measure *38*. If performed as written, measure *38* tends to be heard as an afterbeat to measure *37*, as the weak end of a two-measure group begun at measure *37* (Ex. 3a).[30]

In his revision Beethoven maintains the ambiguity of patterning previously established by means of the conflict between the accent patterns in the rhythmic grouping of the cello part and that of the first violin (m. 30ff., Version 2). The cello continues its strong-weak swing ♩ ♫♫ | ♩ ♩ ♩ | ♩ ♪ ♪ | ♩ ♩ ♩ |, while at measure 37 there is an elision in phrasing in the first violin (Ex. 3b). Beethoven's deletion of the sforzando at measure 37 allows us to hear the first violin part initially as the close of a three-measure group, beginning at measure 35, and subsequently as the first measure in a group that is two measures long. Thus, in Version 2 there is rhythmic instability where there is momentary relative harmonic stability and vice versa. Measure 38 moves across the bar-line melodically but is relatively stable harmonically. At measure 37 the cello patterning may be heard as a continuation of its previous patterning, with measure 37 relatively more mobile and measure 38 more stable. The greater conflict among strong and weak measures in Version 2 is indicated in the diagrams of Example 3.

28. Obviously, I disagree with Roger Sessions's implied analysis of the opening two measures as moving from weak, or upbeat (m. 1), to strong, or downbeat (m. 2); see *The Musical Experience* (Princeton, 1958), p. 13. Indeed, it seems quite conceivable that there will be disagreement among musicians and scholars until the end of time about the way we hear—or should perform and hear—the opening phrase of this movement. Although this is not the place for a tract on how and why we hear the opening phrase as we do, it seems appropriate to give a few reasons for my own stance that the initial motion is essentially from strong, or downbeat (m. 1), to weak, or upbeat (m. 2): (1) the fact of "first-ness," supported by a unison attack and continuation, and with no other event contravening the impulse of this first measure; (2) the strength of durational accent as compared with the second measure, particularly if the entire first measure is understood as an ornamentation of the initial pitch (F); (3) the clarity with which we understand F to be a tonic (stable) after we hear C as the fifth of the scale (less stable) in the second measure.

Here, were it not for the strong coordination of accents in the three upper parts, the turn motive might readily be heard as beginning-accented, as it is in Version 2, because it is the only motive that *begins* at measure 30 and because until that moment no pattern has been articulated (in any parts) for one whole measure (i.e., since the tonic authentic cadence at m. 29). Moreover, the figure was previously understood as a beginning-accented pattern (i.e., m. 1, strong; m. 2, weak).

Example 3

Clarification and regularity of rhythm accommodate increased harmonic activity.

While the revisions in measures 29–41 involved a change from rhythmic clarity to rhythmic ambiguity, those in the next phase of the transition (mm. 41–49) involve precisely the opposite: namely, change from a kind of rhythmic ambiguity approaching confusion in

Measures 41–49

29. It would seem that in Version 1 Beethoven took his cues for the articulation of the inner parts at measure *31ff.* from measure *29ff.*, where the patterning first occurs. Although it serves as a natural connective when carried into measure *31ff.* (as it is in Version 1), this patterning ultimately negates the vamp-like aspect of measures *29–31*. This is so because in retrospect measure *29* in Version 1 is not sufficiently differentiated from the following measures to be heard as "outside." Also, because of the harmony at measure *35* in Version 1, Beethoven cannot maintain the pattern of articulation he has set up (mm. *31* and *33*) on the first beat in the viola and second violin. What he does to accommodate the harmony in Version 1 is somewhat abrupt for the midst of this passage.

30. The weak beat (m. *38*) is fused with the strong one (m. *37*) by the tie. The eighth-note upbeat to measure *39* in the cello somewhat mitigates the groupings within the bar-line, but not enough.

Version 1 to rhythmic clarity in Version 2 (Ex. 4). The clarity and regularity in Version 2 accommodate an increase in harmonic activity (m. 41ff.); that is, rhythmic regularity allows attention more fully to be directed to the harmonic process that is preeminent here.[31] The changes in these measures will be discussed in relation to the ways in which they enhance the high-level sequence of movement to G, as the dominant of C and the immediate goal of the process begun at measure 29.

Rhythmic structure is the most problematic aspect of the passage between measures *41* and *49* in Version 1. Measure *41* is a beginning (as well as a cadence for the previous phrase), with a new harmony and a new figure-ground relationship (the E♭ in the viola and in the broken-chord figuration in the second violin function as a pedal point). But when the

Example 4

first violin reenters with the melody, measure *42* also sounds like a beginning (again). How, then, does one hear the patterning of the first two beats of measure *42* if what follows is heard as in Example 5?

31. In the first part of the transition, rhythmic ambiguity and pedal-point action produce instability, while here (m. 41ff.) Beethoven's revisions make harmonic instability the focus. For a general discussion of the relationships of constancy to change among parameters and how such relationships affect our perception of patterning, see Leonard B. Meyer, *Explaining Music: Essays and Explorations* (Berkeley, 1973), p. 54.

Example 5

Rhythmically, the first beats of measure *42* in the first violin are not easily assimilated into any pattern.[32] If, on the other hand, the patterning in measures *42* and *43* is heard as trochaic (—◡) within the measure, then the G and the eighth rest on the first beat of measure *44* are puzzling in relation to what follows immediately (Ex. 6):

Example 6

For, although in prospect the G may be heard as the beginning of a trochaic group, it cannot be heard as such in retrospect, because of the rest and because of the leap to E♭ that follows both the G and the rest.

If, despite the problems outlined above, the patterning in measures *42–44* is perceived as ◡ — ◡ (a patterning that is clearly realized in Version 2), it is only weakly so. Because the beginning of measure *42* is strongly marked as the *beginning* of a pattern, the end of the figure cannot easily be heard as an upbeat (Ex. 7).

Example 7

The neutral eighth-note figuration of the second violin does nothing to clarify rhythmic grouping; indeed, the bowing and the figuration in the second violin reinforce the within-bar rhythm of the first violin, creating a lulling effect.

The two revisions that most affect the rhythmic structure of the passage from measure 41 to 47 are: (1) the tying of the C in the first violin from measure 41 to 42, and (2) the addition of the appoggiatura on beat 1 in measures 43 and 45. The tying of the C is combined with the action in other parameters to make measure 41 a beginning in *all* parameters. One small but noteworthy difference between the two versions in this respect is the cessation of the eighth-note pulsation at measure 41 (Version 2). This contributes to the articulation of measure 41 as a beginning.

32. The C at measure *41* in Version 1 can be heard as a continuation of the iambic grouping of measures that has been ongoing from measure *29*.

Not only is the beginning of the passage made clear, but the tied C (mm. 41–42) also establishes the end of measure 42 as an upbeat to the beginning of measure 43 (similarly with the D♭ in the second violin, mm. 43–44). Together with the stresses that the addition of the appoggiaturas E♭ (beginning of m. 43) and F (beginning of m. 45) provide, the tied C (as well as the D♭, mm. 43–44) affects a high-level pattern, as shown in Example 8.

Example 8

Moreover, in contrast to the first part of the transition (i.e., mm. 29–37), the turn figure (in the viola, mm. 41, 43, 45) and the appoggiatura figure (first violin, mm. 43 and 45) are congruent; their accent patterns are the same (Ex. 4). Their congruence is heightened by the revised second violin part, which underlines the anacrustic aspect of the last two beats of measures 42, 44, and 46 and helps to make the rhythmic patterning in the first violin unequivocal. The resultant strong accents on measures 43, 45, and 47 are coordinated with the harmonic changes at these points (that is, every two measures) so that attention is directed to the harmonic process.

Melodic changes complement harmonic processes and create high-level linear continuity.

Melodically, Beethoven's addition of the appoggiatura to measures 43 and 45 in the first violin part (Version 2) links the patterning in these measures to that in the first violin line of measures 31, 33, and 35.[33] This melodic similarity also focuses attention on the harmonic process of the transition: there are not as many new patterns to be related. More important still, the similarity of these measures points up a linear continuity present within the transition in Version 2: namely, the sequence set up at measure 31ff. is broken at measure 34 and resumed at measure 43 (Ex. 9). By spanning foreground events between measures 35 and 43, the sequential patterning at once bonds the entire transition and intensifies a single trajectory to G, as V for C. Unlike Version 1, the presence of the appoggiatura as part of the figure here (cf. the corresponding figure in Version 1, mm. *43* and *45*) creates a contrast with

33. The similarity of these passages will be important in the recapitulation and coda. See below, pp. 79–82, 90–92, and n. 163.

measure 47. Its absence at measure 47 then functions to highlight the change of patterning that takes place—a change to larger units—and to suggest that the sequence itself is about to be broken.

Example 9

Revisions of texture help to signal impending articulation.

Revisions of texture at measures 47–49 (Ex. 4) coordinate with the melodic action, just described, to signal the next important articulation in the transition: the poise on V/V (on G, for C). In Version 2 a rhythmic unison at measure 47 (for the first time since the cadence at mm. 18–20) replaces the texture of Version 1, in which the inner parts continue with an accompanimental pattern that had been set up in the preceding measure (m. *46*). Together with the fact that the basic pulsation in eighth-notes (in mm. *46–47*, Version 1) is undifferentiated from the pulsation that had been ongoing from measure *29*, this lack of immediate textural contrast tends to link measures *47–49* with their preceding measures in Version 1 rather than to heighten their forward connection to the G major chord at measure 49. Further, the acceleration of harmonic rhythm at measures 47–48 is underscored by the change of texture within Version 2 (compare m. 46 with mm. 47–48). This is not the case in Version 1.

Motion toward the second key area is intensified by changes in dynamics, melody, rhythm, and texture.

Measures 49–55

Textural and melodic revisions, along with modifications of dynamics, continue to make the approach to the second key area more mobile in Version 2 (Ex. 10). As compared with the undifferentiated *forte* in Version 1, the sudden *piano* in Version 2 (m. 49, beat 1)[34] dramatizes the arrival at V/V and makes possible the crescendo to *fortissimo*, which intensifies the sweep toward the structural articulation at measure 55. These dynamic modifications are but the first of several revisions that reinforce the anacrustic nature of the motion towards measure 55.

34. In the Breitkopf & Härtel *Gesamtausgabe*, ser. 6, vol. 1, no. 37, the shift from *f* to *p* occurs not on the first beat of the measure, but on the second sixteenth-note in the first violin and on the second half of beat 2 in the second violin and viola; in the cello it does not occur until beat 1 of measure 50.

By comparison, melodic and rhythmic motion across the bar-line (m. *49* to m. *50* and immediately successive bar-lines) is quite closed in Version 1. This is due primarily, though not exclusively, to the patterning of the third beat in measure *49* and in successive measures up to measure *55*. In Version 1 the figure on beat 3 in the first violin (Ex. 10, motive x), as well as the analogous figure in the cello (mm. *50* and *52*), is more spelled out harmonically—outlining [C] V–I$^{\flat 3}$–V—and is a more patently patterned and closed shape than the corresponding figure in Version 2. Because it is merely a neighbor-note figure in Version 2, an alternation of tones (Ex. 10, motive y), the figure is more neutral, open-ended, and less explicit in implying a particular moment of terminus.[35]

Rhythmically, the upbeat patterning in Version 2 (♩ 𝄽 ♫♫ | ♩), in contrast with that in Version 1 (♩ 𝄽 ♫ | ♩), generates more momentum than is stabilized by the downbeat that follows in each case. (In Version 1 the intensified upbeat patterning *is* heard at measures *53–54* in the lower parts.) The result in Version 2 is greater propulsion. The cello's reiteration of G–C/G (mm. *49*, *51*, *53*, and *54*, Version 1) strongly articulates the plagal chord progression (beat 3 to beat 1) and bogs down forward motion. And, while in Version 2 Beethoven seems careful to save the low G *on the beat* (m. 82) for the weightiest cadence of the second key area, in Version 1 he "uses it up" prematurely (mm. *53–54*), so to speak, in the midst of the vamp to the second key area.

Texturally, for the last beat of each measure in measures *49–52* of Version 1, as well as for the first beats in measures *50–55*, double-stops produce a full five-voiced sound. In contrast, the texture in Version 2 is three-part at measures 49 and 51 and four-part in the other measures of the passage (mm. 50, 52, 53, 54). This relative lightness of texture fosters the gradual intensification in the measures immediately preceding measure *55*.[36] Most importantly, Beethoven writes a textural unison in Version 2, at measure 54.

A gradual augmentation of texture and concomitant increase in sonority and dynamic level (as in mm. *49–55*, Version 2) are often hallmarks of the end of a transition in the classic style. The textural unison at measure 54 is just such an indication: as a typical gesture of full textural "verve" before a second key area it signals the important articulation at measure 55.[37] By comparison, the sameness of texture in each measure between measures *49* and *54* in Version 1 generates little if any drive toward the articulation of the beginning of the second key area. The textural unison in Version 2 (m. 54) also has another subtle but important consequence: the effect of a single line produced by the unison provides a smooth transition to the literal solo line in the first violin (m. 55). Unlike Version 1, where marked

---

35. In Version 1 the figure on the last beat of each measure from measure *49* to *54* seems more idiomatic for piano than for violin or cello, particularly at a fast tempo.

36. See the comment on dynamics in relation to textural changes, p. 15.

37. For a discussion of textural action in relation to structure and, in particular, the concept of a "period of verve," see my Ph.D. dissertation, "The *Quatuor Concertant* in Paris in the Latter Half of the Eighteenth Century" (Stanford University, 1971), pp. 197–274. There I discuss the theorist De Momigny's notion of a "period of verve," as found in his *Cours Complet d'harmonie et de composition*, vol. 2 (Paris, 1805–06), pp. 397–99.

Example 10

textural contrast between measures *54* and *55* creates separation, texture in Version 2 creates a processive connection.

This connection seems symptomatic of Beethoven's concern to keep the motion into the second key area as fluid and open as possible—very much on a continuing "upswing." That this is so can be inferred from the change he made in Version 2 at the juncture of measure 55, where he weakens the articulation of G by clearing out the chord specification and by replacing it simply with a doubled G, which is clearly more mobile than the full chord (Version 1). Moreover, in Version 2 he has approached the G from essentially the *same* harmony, one on G (in a rising scale); in Version 1, on the other hand, the established progression across each bar-line, from a chord on C to one on G, is maintained. Paradoxically, then, the articulation in Version 2 is at once more clearly marked, through contrast with preceding measures, yet is less decisive than that in Version 1. The relatively smooth motion (Version 2) from the transition to the second key area is entirely in keeping with the tune that gives profile to the new key area.

As with many of the modifications in earlier segments, the revisions of the second key area contribute to a more kinetic process from the beginning (m. *55*) to the area of arrival for the entire exposition (m. *109*/101). The formal structure of the second key area in Version 2 is also different from that in Version 1. In Version 2 the reduction in the number of closural articulations (mm. *72–109*/72–101), as well as a telescoping of eight measures (between mm. *72* and *86*, Version 1), creates a more dynamic and cohesive motion to the emphatic confirmation of C major at measure 84/*92*. The discussion of the second key area will be divided as follows:

> Measures *55–72*: opening segment
> Measures *72–92*/72–84: telescoping in Version 2
> > mm. *72–86*/72–78
> > mm. *86–92*/78–84
> Measures *92–122*/84–114: closing area
> > mm. *92–109*/84–101
> > mm. *109–22*/101–14

Measures
55–72

Bonding: changes in instrumentation, surface rhythm, and part-writing enhance continuity and coherence.

In the context of this movement, the profile tune for the second key area (mm. 57–72) certainly has its own unmistakably defined character, but it is not a very characteristic second key-area tune (Ex. 12).[39] It would seem that the patent symmetry—virtual squareness—in the phrase structure of Version 1 may reflect Beethoven's awareness of traditional treatments of this segment. But this version seems *too* regular: a decidedly additive 4 + 4 + 4 + 4 measure-grouping detracts from large-scale coherence. This construction is supplanted in Version 2 by an 8 + 8 = 16 measure-grouping, a result of subtler melodic construction, refinement of part-writing and texture, and an intensified cadence at measure 72. Perhaps most importantly, the revision bonds the entire sixteen measures more strongly. Although the individual revisions are intricately linked, I shall discuss them separately.

The increased clarity of the large-scale (8 + 8 = 16 measures) phrase relationships in Version 2 is a consequence of several factors. Chief among these are the revised surface rhythm in phrase 2 (mm. 61–64), the revised order of instrumental entries in phrases 3 (mm. 65–68) and 4 (mm. 69–72), and the resultant changes in part-writing. First, the role of surface rhythm: in Version 1 the sameness of eighth-note motion in successive phrases until

---

38. Because Beethoven adds and deletes measures in the revision from measure 72 on, the measure numbers of corresponding passages in the two versions are not the same. To make references to corresponding passages clear, citations of measure numbers for both versions will be given; for example: mm. *55–122*/55–114 is to be read as "measures *55* to *122* in Version 1, corresponding to measures 55 to 114 in Version 2." Wherever feasible Version 1 will be referred to first.

39. For a discussion of the "Passo Caratteristico" in the second key area, see Bathia Churgin, "Francesco Galeazzi's Description (1796) of Sonata Form," *Journal of the American Musicological Society* 21 (1968): 181–99.

---

the final one contributes to the additive character of the phrase organization. Beethoven mitigates this character in Version 2 by replacing the eighth-notes with quarter-notes in the violin parts of phrase 2. This changed surface rhythm helps to differentiate phrase 2 from both the immediately preceding and immediately following phrases and to articulate a grouping of phrases 1 plus 2, and 3 plus 4. More importantly, the surface rhythm of the end of phrase 2 (mm. 63–64) now matches that of the end of phrase 4 (mm. 71–72),[40] and this similarity over a musical distance helps to relate these measures to one another as ends of phrase-groups.[41]

The revised instrumentation in phrase 3 (mm. 65–68) of Version 2—beginning the main line in the cello rather than the second violin, as in Version 1—also contributes to the larger phrase-grouping in several ways. First, because the first violin (mm. 67–68) now has the prominent "counterline" (which, in phrase 1 of both versions, had been in the lowest voices), a kind of high-level symmetrical pattern of changing-note figures emerges between the ends of phrases. That is, the ends of phrases 1 and 2 taken together, and phrases 3 and 4 taken together, now relate in two complementary sequential patterns that emphasize the 8 + 8 measure-grouping (Ex. 11b).[42] Once the patterning of measures 60 and 64 is realized in this context, the motion from C to B at measure 68 strongly implies that D to C will follow, as it does. In Version 1, when G moves to F for the second time at the end of phrase 3 (just as it had at the end of phrase 1), there is no clear implication of what will follow;[43] in this respect, large-scale patterning simply breaks down at the end of the phrase-group in Version 1 (Ex. 11a).[44] Like any ordered sequence, the complementary patterns in Version 2, shown in Example 11b, also heighten process; the much stronger motion from leading tone to tonic in Version 1 (mm. *71–72*) tends to create closure.

Example 11

40. Even in Version 1, of course, the end of phrase 4 had been in quarter-note motion.

41. Beethoven himself seems to have been uncomfortable with phrase 2 in Version 1, for he revised it in the recapitulation of the *same* version, changing the surface rhythm to quarter-note motion in measures *233–35*. He carried this "ready-made" revision from the recapitulation of Version 1 into the exposition of Version 2, but never went back to change the corresponding segment of the exposition in Version 1. See the text, pp. 86 and 100–101.

42. Although the leading tone, B, is present for the cadence (m. 71) in Version 2, it is so only briefly. The more prominent pitch on this third beat is the D. The metric placement of the end of the sequence is adjusted to make a forceful cadence on the first beat of the measure.

43. One assumes that the patterning of phrases 1 and 2 will not keep repeating!

44. Even the G–F that ends phrase 3 is not very clear in this version because it is obscured by the high G pedal tone in the first violin (mm. *67–68*). This glaring "textural error" was doubtless one reason for Beethoven's change in the arrangement of the parts in Version 2. And it was perhaps this "mistake" that also led to the omission of the G pedal altogether in phrase 1 of Version 2. For the G pedal in the first violin of phrase 3 in Version 1 results from the maintenance of similarity from phrase 1 to phrase 3 but with a change in the relationship of the concerting parts (*within* Version 1).

A second effect of the revised instrumentation is more important still (Ex. 12). Although in *both* versions the main line of each successive phrase is carried by a different instrument, in the true concertante style, in Version 1 there is a partial effect of timbral backtracking when phrase 3 begins in the second violin. In Version 2, on the other hand, a progressive change in sonority (at the beginning of each phrase) creates a certain continuity through the phrase-group and gives the passage an effect of being through-composed.[45] The kind of progressive differentiation of textures within the sixteen measures, created especially by the revised instrumentation for phrase 3 in Version 2, coordinates with the evolving change in sonority to contribute to the integration of the entire sixteen-measure unit.[46]

The intensification of the cadence at measure 72: the roles of melody, rhythm, and harmony.

The most important factor in the cohesion of the sixteen measures in Version 2 is the sweeping intensification of the cadence at measure 72. This results from a conjunction of numerous revisions.[47] Problematic aspects of harmony and line in Version 1 will be considered first.

The final phrase in Version 1 (Ex. 12, mm. *69–72*) is very awkward because Beethoven keeps the correspondence with the main line of phrase 2 through the tone G♯ (m. *62* cf. m. *70*), which functions as an enhancement of VI in both phrases. In order to arrive at dominant harmony for the cadence in C (as opposed to the half-cadence in phrase 2), Beethoven moves the line quickly to the sixth degree of the scale. In so doing, he forces the line into a sequence (G♯–A, F♯–G) in measures *70–71*. A sequence is not only misplaced for the cadential moment, but it also sets up a hemiola in the cello line (three measures of 2/4 rather than two of 3/4). Completely unprepared, and not joined by the other voices, the hemiola in the cello alone seems forced. The G♯ (m. *70*) is pivotal in its melodic function: it groups with the preceding measures as a continuation of the descending triad beginning on F; it also groups with the next tone, A, in beginning the sequential pattern (mm. *70–71*). Thus, even the dominant function for C, initially outlined by the descending triad F–D–B (m. *69*), is partly superseded as the chain of thirds continues downward to G♯, which retrospectively functions as VII for VI. There is, then, only one true measure (m. *71*) of dominant harmony immediately before the tonic cadence in the new key.

In Version 2 Beethoven deals with this problem by beginning phrase 4 with a motion from G to A♭ rather than from E to F (as in Version 1), and this change has several significant consequences. One is that the G♯ in Version 2, which was problematic in the final phrase of Version 1, is readily and immediately interpreted as A♭ in a context of C minor. As a result, one can hear virtually all of phrase 4 as dominant function with strong cadential implications. The main line itself (second violin) outlines the tensional diminished-seventh chord on B. (Indeed, Beethoven prepared this intensification at the end of phrase 3 by including the tone A♭ as part of the VII$_3^4$ harmony on beat 1, measure 68, replacing the more stable V$_5^6$ at the end of phrase 3 in Version 1.)

Another consequence of beginning phrase 4 with G–A♭ (rather than E–F) is that this progression cues us that the ensuing motion will *not* "match" that of phrase 2 in its internal structure, as indeed it does not. In some sense, the turn to the minor sixth of the scale, along with the "new" melodic patterning (as compared with phrase 2), is itself a sign of the very intensification that follows. Before further considering the intensification of the cadence, however, a third consequence of the revised main line should be mentioned.

45. Of course, it might be argued that the similarity in sound between first and second violin in the beginnings of the first and third phrases of Version 1 emphasizes the large phrase structure; but here, I think, the effect of a through-composed sonority (Version 2) is a way of bonding the entire sixteen-measure group while articulation takes place in other parameters.

Example 12

Revisions of instrumentation are also related to details of rhythm and part-writing in various ways. For instance, the length of the tone B♮ in the cello at measure *60* (cf. viola, Version 2) probably led Beethoven to begin phrase 2 on E (with ♪ as an anacrusis rather than ♫, as in Version 2). And this, in turn, would have affected the construction in phrase 4 (end of m. *68*).

46. Other reasons, primarily harmonic, for the revised instrumentation are discussed below. A comparison of textures here and in the recapitulation will be considered on p. 86.

47. This intensification is also significant in relation to immediately subsequent changes. See pp. 25–28.

In Version 2 the revised line of phrase 4 subtly suggests the potential of an antecedent-consequent phrase relationship between phrases 1 and 4, with phrases 2 and 3 being heard, retrospectively, as a kind of trope or interpolation between phrases 1 and 4 (see Ex. 13a).

Example 13

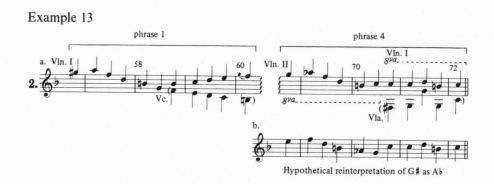

Hypothetical reinterpretation of G♯ as A♭

Beethoven could have interpreted the G♯ as A♭, even had phrase 4 begun like phrase 2, without the notable change of line (see Ex. 13b). But this potential antecedent-consequent relationship would not have emerged. And despite the fact that phrases 1 and 4 (taken, as it were, side by side) are not entirely antecedent-consequent in their character, Beethoven's revision of the main line of phrase 4 tends to corroborate our perception that phrase 2 somehow might have been a consequent for phrase 1, in which case this segment would have consisted of a pair of antecedent-consequent phrases: phrases 1 and 2 as one antecedent-consequent phrase and phrases 3 and 4 as the other.[48] This potential structure was realized in neither version largely because it was thwarted by the open ending of phrase 2 (Ex. 12). Throughout the profile theme Beethoven seems to have played on the fact that the second phrase did not, as it might have, turn out to be the consequent of the first. In this context of a succession of balanced phrases set as statement-and-response, too many open endings—three in a row—make this theme "odd." The revision of the main line of phrase 4 shows us just what has been so odd, what the play has been "about."[49]

48. I posit this despite the fact that the most common use of "antecedent-consequent phrase-group" refers to two phrases that begin in the same way and end differently: i.e., the first, or antecedent, phrase is open; the second, or consequent, phrase is closed.

49. Of course, in both versions a kind of large-scale antecedent-consequent phrase relationship emerges, if the first two phrases are taken together as antecedent and the second two as consequent. When phrase 3 begins as phrase 1 did, we listen for a relationship linking phrases 3 and 4 to phrases 1 and 2; and we are given it in both versions. But in Version 1, because the closing motions of phrase 4 come late, awkwardly, and perfunctorily (see text, p. 20), the total antecedent-consequent structure is weak; Version 2 is more strongly bonded.

Returning to the intensification of the cadence: in Version 2 the final cadence of the phrase-group is begun sooner than it is either in Version 1 or in any of the three preceding phrases of Version 2. The internal structure of the phrase is considerably modified as compared either with phrase 2 (m. 62 ff.) in this version or with the analogous fourth phrase in Version 1 (m. *70 ff.*). Modifications of texture figure importantly here. The counterline in the first violin, whose entrance in each of the three preceding phrases (within Version 2) has been associated with a motion to the half-cadence (the caesura on V), now begins a full measure earlier than it had in the preceding phrase (that is, at m. 69, beat 3, rather than m. 70, beat 3) and pushes toward the cadence at measure 72 for that much longer. In Version 1 the counterline enters at the same moment it did in phrase 2. The imitative counterpoint between second violin and viola at measure 69 combines with the longer counterline, the dominant harmony of the main melodic patterning, and the augmented texture to heighten the motion toward the cadence at measure 72. The revised main line and its placement in the second violin also highlight and increase precadential tension when the high A♭ in the first violin (mm. 69–70), sounded against the B of the second violin (beat 1, m. 70), creates a prominent and biting instability.

A small but significant rhythmic revision of the very end of the final phrase also strengthens the cadence and furthers the integration of the sixteen measures in Version 2. In Version 1 the rhythmic conformance of measure *72* with all the preceding phrase ends on weak beats contributes to the additive construction of the four phrases.[50] The rather gauche octave drop (beat 2, m. *72*), which effects the rhythmic parallelism here, weakens the force, as well as the momentum, of the cadence on the first beat of measure *72*. Because it does not differentiate the close of phrase 4 from that of preceding phrases the rhythmic parallelism fails to clarify the formal articulation. Further, the octave drop detracts from the articulation at measure *72* because it is heard as a redundant afterbeat to a goal already reached on beat 1 in the measure.[51]

In Version 2 Beethoven strengthens the downbeat. Not only does he eliminate the weak afterbeat of Version 1, but he also greatly heightens the anacrustic quality of motion before the downbeat at measure 72. He changes the rhythm of the violin parts from ♩♩♩♩♩♩♩♩ in Version 1 to ♩♩♩♩♩♩♩♩ in Version 2; and he reinforces this change by the anacrustic anticipation of the rinforzando C (m. 71) on the third beat of measure 70.

In one sense, then, although the weak beat in Version 1 leaves the final phrase open, it also absorbs and dissipates some of the accumulated momentum. In Version 2, on the other hand, the cadence at measure 72 is a strong point of articulation; yet paradoxically, at the same time, the accumulated energy has no chance to dissipate.

50. This is so despite the fact that, for the first time in the phrase-group, there is surface-rhythmic differentiation of the counterline.

51. In this respect, the "similarity" actually contrasts with the three earlier "feminine endings."

By intensifying cadential harmony (and texture)

Version 1:	mm.	*69–70*	*71*	*72*
(C)		VII/VI(VI)–V$^6_5$/V	V($^{6-5}_{4-3}$)	I$^{\flat 3}$

Version 2:	mm.	69–70	71	72
(c)		VII^7–(I)–VII^7/V	V($^{6-5}_{4-3}$)	I$^{\natural 3}$

as well as by interrupting the normal "schedule" of events in the final phrase of the phrase-group (the early entrance of the counterline), Beethoven escalates not only the force but also the momentum of arrival at measure 72 in Version 2. C major arrives with freshness and in a specially satisfying way after the piquant touch of C minor. In a way, the major is refreshed even before it is heard as a tonic cadence for the very first time (see below, p. 26, for discussion of Version 1).

Momentum escalates beyond the cadence.

The momentum across the cadence in Version 2 is also enhanced by the absence of the cello as a bass line for the final phrase; in the revision, the viola provides the bass for the cadence at measure 72 (Ex. 12). Most importantly, this arrangement in Version 2 reserves the sound of the cello for the weightier cadence at measure 84. In short, the instrumentation here helps to delay a more complete arrival in the second key and fosters a longer-range trajectory from the opening of the second key area to the emphatic arrival of C major at measure 84.[52] Noteworthy, too, is that after its absence from the final phrase, the cello reappears (m. 72) with the first melodic pattern of the *next* phase of movement. Particularly because of its high register, the cello helps to mark this moment as a beginning.

Small dynamic revisions also promote movement toward and across the cadence. In Version 1 only the cello has a crescendo to a *piano*; the other voices have a ⏤⏤ ⏥⏥ (mm. *70–71*) to a *piano*. In Version 2 all three voices making the cadence have a crescendo, including a rinforzando (beat 1, m. 71, violins), to a *piano* (m. 72). In denying the expected dynamic emphasis, this abrupt dynamic change has the *effect* of a deceptive cadence. Ongoing motion is thus increased.

52. Aside from the reasons given (in the text) for the cello's lead (and not that of the second violin) in phrase 3 of Version 2, it would also seem that Beethoven may have realized that placing the cello last in the concertante distribution of the main line (as in Version 1) preordains that the cadence at measure 72 will be heavier than is suitable.

In addition, in Version 2 the surface rhythm in the first and second violins (m. 71) ♩ ♪♩(♩ ♪) more closely resembles that of the turn figure ♩ ♪♪♫(♩ ♪) in the next phase of movement than does the corresponding motion (quarter-note) in Version 1. This makes for a subtle processive rhythmic connection across the cadence, lessening the formal break between events before measure 72 and those after it.

The spillover of momentum, as well as other aspects of the changes in the opening segment of the second key area (that is, mm. 57–72), may be explained not only in terms of the local syntax just considered, but also in terms of the changes Beethoven made in the subsequent passage; that is, later changes (those from mm. 72 to 77, Version 2) may have influenced earlier ones (namely, mm. 69–72 and, reflexively, perhaps even some in m. 58ff.).[53]

Telescoping in Version 2 throws the cadence at measure 78 into sharp relief and tightens movement to the end of the exposition.

*Measures
72–86
72–78*

The cardinal change Beethoven makes in the section from measure 72 to the end of the exposition is a telescoping of the passage from measures *72* to *86* in Version 1 (see Ex. 14).[54] In telescoping, he excises eight full measures, including one of the two emphatic authentic cadences in C major/minor (m. *86*, Version 1, corresponds to m. 78, Version 2). The result, in Version 2, is a tightened trajectory to the strongest presentation of C major to this point in the movement (m. 84/*92*) and an altogether more dynamic and cohesive movement from measure 72 to the end of the exposition.

The matter of precisely which measures are excised from Version 1 is not as simple as it may at first seem.[55] In reducing fourteen measures to six (Version 1 to Version 2), Beethoven takes some elements from measure *72ff.* and some from measure *80ff.* of Version 1.

---

53. If one were attempting to explain the genesis of the quartet, evidence from the last autograph and sketches to the revision (presumed nonexistent for this passage) would be especially helpful here (see p. 3 and n. 12). One would try to answer such questions as:

(1) Did Beethoven first excise the eight measures in C minor and then change measures 69–72 to incorporate C minor and the intensification of the cadence?

(2) Did he first work for the major-minor contrast in the segment between measures 69 and 72, and then, having achieved it within the passage, excise the C minor plateau because it was redundant? That is, did the new cadence-phrase do the work of the entire C minor segment, as it were, besides tightening the trajectory to measure 84?

54. In order to show what is telescoped following measure *72* in Version 1, Example 14 aligns measure 72ff. of Version 2 with *two* sets of measures in Version 1: measure *72ff.* and measure *80ff.*

55. Wedig, for example, simply asserts that "the eight-measure C minor episode after measure 71 is eliminated," in "Beethovens Streichquartett op. 18, nr. 1," p. 17.

Primarily because of mode (major), chord progression, and some aspects of the two outer lines, measures *80–86* of Version 1 correspond mainly to measures *72–78*, Version 2. Beethoven also incorporates two salient aspects of texture and sonority from the same passage in Version 1: the cello in its high register, with the turn motive as an ornamental ground (V pedal point), and the viola as a true bass. From the C minor "plateau" (mm. *72–80*, Version 1), however, Beethoven takes the basic texture as well as the main melodic continuity.[56] Thus, while measures *72–78* in Version 2 are most readily understood as variants of measures *80–86* in Version 1, they are not exclusively so.

The fusion of aspects of measures *72–80* and *80–85* of Version 1 in the revision can be understood in terms of what is "wrong" with Version 1. Most strikingly, the C minor segment (mm. *72–80*) separates out from any long-range arc of action as a kind of independent block. It is framed by two strong periodic cadences in the new key (the dominant), each "deceptive" in its mode: the first (m. *72*) is prepared in the major but cadences to C minor; the second (m. *80*) is prepared in the minor but cadences to C major.[57] In addition to the strong cadence to C major (m. *80*), the bold contrasts in mode, texture, and melodic and rhythmic activity beginning at measure *80* also tend to reinforce the sectional quality of the immediately preceding eight measures. The strong closure of the eight-measure segment from measures *72* to *80* in Version 1 calls for contrast. Such sharp contrast is not needed, however, in Version 2; Beethoven is able to use the texture of measure *72ff.*, Version 1, for Version 2 simply because he has not already used it up, as he has by measure *80*, Version 1. The new "busy" and polarized texture of measure *80*, Version 1, would have been far too abrupt at measure 72, Version 2.

Further, in Version 1, as a result of register and timbre, the differentiation of accompaniment and ground (viola and cello) from the main lines of action (carried by the violins) creates pronounced articulations at measures *81*, *83*, and *85*. Because the distinctly different material of the upper voices alternates with the turn motive in the cello, these measures relate more to one another than to the immediately preceding or following measures; consequently, the passage seems overarticulated. In his fusion of elements from measures *72ff.* and *80ff.*, Beethoven's choice of melodic action (with an important registral change to be discussed below) corresponding to that at measure *72ff.*, Version 1 (rather than that of m. *80*) makes for a tighter continuity from measure to measure. Despite the "ground" function of the turn motive on G in the cello (mm. 72, 74, 76), its rhythmic similarity to the main line in the first violin creates a dialogue between the two.[58]

The choice of rhythmic activity corresponding to measure *72ff.* in Version 1 (not m. *80ff.*) would seem to have been made with a view to the passage at measure 78 in Version 2 (= m. *86*, Version 1; see Ex. 15). For in Version 1 the sixteenth-note pulsation in the low register of the viola (m. *80ff.*, Ex. 14) prematurely agitates the texture—speeds up the rate of surface activity—and tends to preempt the escalation of activity for the cadence. In Version 2 (m. *72ff.*), however, by using the surface rhythm and texture from measure *72* of Version 1 instead of measure *80*, Beethoven reserves the increased surface activity for the giant anacrusis to the cadence. This action is coordinated with a dramatic shift in articulation at

---

56. Except for mode, the harmonic progression is initially the same in both versions, but, as indicated above in the text, it is also exactly the same in measures *80–83* of Version 1.

57. The piquant chord disposition in the (C): V/IV–IV progression in measures *77–78* of Version 1 heightens the effect of the cadence at measure *80*; this progression has no counterpart in Version 2.

58. That is, the ground and melody figures in alternate measures are similar enough, without being identical, that the patterning does not separate out or break down into one-measure units.

Example 14

measure 77 (that is, just prior to the beginning of the large rhythmic upbeat in measure 78). The break at measure 77—a function of the shift in register, the disruption of regular pattern continuation (E[B] – F[C♯] → G) and, subsequently, the stepped-up surface rhythm—signals the change in action at measure 78/86. The melodic gap (Version 2) from the C♯ (m. 76) to the high B♭ (m. 77, first violin) heightens the tension of the unstable VII[7] chord, which functions as a dominant for the chord on D at measure 78 (cf. m. *85*, Version 1, beginning just as m. *83* does, in the first violin). This skip of a diminished seventh in an outer voice, with its top member, B♭, a strong structural tone, emphasized by the *forte*, provides a large thrust—a kind of dramatic anacrusis to the anacrusis—to the II[6] chord (on D) that forms the beginning of the broad cadential formula (mm. 78–84): II[6]–V–V[7]–I. This dramatization of the approach is simply missing in Version 1 because the action in measure *85* is not significantly different from that at measure *81* or *83*.

It is clear that Beethoven was dissatisfied with the register in Version 1— primarily the high register of the main line in all measures from *72* to *85*. In telescoping this passage for Version 2 he moved the register of the highest line down (in whatever material he reused). His commitment to the high register in Version 1 immediately following the first authentic cadence in C minor (m. *72*) ultimately robs the high C of some of its structural force. This is because the same high C is reiterated several times in structural positions (mm. *76, 78, 80*) very soon thereafter. In Version 2 the high C (m. 72) is never again heard as a strong structural tone in the exposition; it retains its original focal position.

The approach to the II^6 chord on D (in the key of C), which functions as a prolonged harmonic and rhythmic anacrusis to the cadence at measure 84/92, is notably altered by registral changes. In Version 1 the high B and C♯ (mm. *82* and *84*) imply motion to a *high* D (at m. *86*), but the registral break (the octave drop) disrupts the linear sweep and direction to measure *86*. Instead of continuing mounting tension, the low D slackens it.[59] In Version 2, however, the tones B–C♯–D (mm. 74, 76, 78) are heard in a *single* register and form one linear progression that spotlights the sweep toward measure 78.

Measures
86–92
78–84

Changes in dynamics, texture, instrumentation, and foreground harmony strengthen the anacrusis to the cadence.

The choppiness that the registral break creates in the linear trajectory of Version 1 (see above), is not only continued but is increased in the measures that constitute the anacrusis to the cadence at measure *92* (Ex. 15). It is increased by the occurrence of at least three conflicting groupings of beats in measures *86–89*, a result of the sforzandi (mm. *86, 87, 88*) and the chords (beat 2, mm. *87, 88*). These groupings include: (1) the established meter which, because of prior organization, tends to continue itself; (2) a succession of two-beat units projected by melodic patterning, beginning with the first beat of measure *86*; (3) three-beat units, beginning with each sforzando chord on the second beat of each measure. The second of these patterings is the one that "wants" to dominate, and in Version 2 it

59. Or, the other way around, the high B and C♯ are unsatisfactory in relation to the D (m. *86*) that Beethoven does seem to have wanted in that register, for it is the one pitch in the main line that remains unchanged in Version 2.

Example 15

does so. In Version 1 the pattern of three-beat units is mainly confusing; this is particularly so in its third occurrence (m. *88*, beat 2ff.) where the threefold ambiguity created by the simultaneous articulation of conflicting patterns ultimately detracts from the effect of anacrusis (mm. *86–89*). The anacrustic character is lost, so to speak, in the listener's attempt to grasp patterning.

In Version 2 the removal of the sforzando on the second beats of measures 78–80 (cf. mm. *86–88*, Version 1) and the chords in measures 79 and 80 (cf. mm. *87–88*, Version 1) allows the duple patterning of the melodic line to be perceived in a kind of metric counterpoint with the ongoing triple meter. The chord (without sforzando) on the second beat of measure 78 in Version 2 tends to equalize beats 1 and 2, to set off the patterning of the two-beat unit, and to direct attention to the beat-grouping shown in Example 16a rather than that in Example 16b; that is, unlike measure *86* in Version 1 the second beat is *not* the thetic part of an iambic group but, rather, the group of two beats is a closed pattern: beat: ⌐͞1 ͝2⌐ .

Example 16

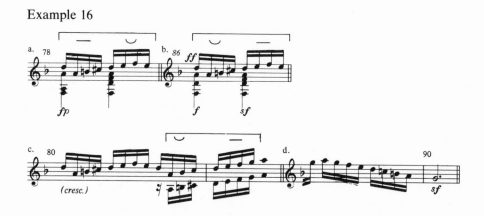

Thus, for the entire passage in Version 2, understatement in dynamics and harmony helps to bond two overlapping patterns—one created by the ongoing triple meter and the other by the melodic patterning—in a single giant anacrusis composed of two macromeasures of three beats each (that is, three double-beats); see Example 15, Version 2.

By avoiding the interpretation of the two-beat pattern as it is shown in Example 16b (a latent possibility all along)[60] Beethoven can use this new interpretation of the pattern to enhance the grand gesture of "verve" preceding the cadence proper at measure 84 (Ex. 15). Thus, the unison doubling begins, not on the D, which would have begun yet another (a fifth) unit of the two-beat pattern, but on the A, the second sixteenth-note of the group (Ex. 16c). This doubling makes the notes A–B–C♯ an anacrusis and directs motion across the bar-line, emphasizing D as V/V; significantly, as a break with preceding patterning, the augmentation of the texture combines with the crescendo to quickly prepare the next motion. Put another way, the change in patterning at the end of measure 80 not only functions as a kind of "mini-sign" that breaks the spell of preceding repetitions, but also spotlights the move to dominant harmony. There is no such preparation in the analogous

60. Another possibility latent in the patterning—namely, the continuation and completion of the scale on the high A (reached by moving through G instead of returning to E)—is also realized at the beginning of measure 81.

passage in Version 1, where the "warning passage" is shorter (see Ex. 16d) and not dramatized by texture as it is in Version 2 (Ex. 15).

Moreover, the doublings in Version 2 (m. 81 and upbeat), particularly that of the cello line, provide a felicitous position for approach to the low G. In Version 1 this G occurred "prematurely" (mm. *54–55*). In Version 2, on the other hand, G (m. 82) is heard in this structural position for the *first* time in the movement. By reserving the low G until measure 82 in Version 2, Beethoven intensifies cadential arrival in C major (m. 84). Further, the low G here sets up the right position for an *upward* sweep toward the cadence (as compared with the downward scale-motion in m. *90* of Version 1). The rising line is more anacrustic, the whole motion more airborne,[61] in keeping with the more anacrustic quality of the entire second key area in Version 2.

That Beethoven was interested in enhancing the motion to the cadence at measure 84 seems corroborated by revisions in dynamics; for these revisions coordinate with the others. In Version 1 the dynamic level of the whole passage is *fortissimo* (m. *86ff.*), punctuated by sforzandi. In Version 2 the dynamic level is *piano* (initiated by a *forte-piano* at m. 78), with a crescendo from the end of measure 79 that is reinforced by instrumental doublings and the second crescendo marking at the end of measure 80. These modifications in dynamics contribute to the cumulative motion to the cadence in Version 2. Whereas the sforzando of measure *90* in Version 1 (cf. m. 82, Version 2) is heard as just one of many in the preceding passage, and is thus not especially marked for attention, the *forte* reached via a crescendo in Version 2 increases cohesion in the entire passage (mm. 78–84).

Closing Area
(Measures *92–122*/**84–114**)

Registral revisions promote internal coherence and dramatize the most formal cadence in the second key area.

It is primarily register that is revised in the passage that leads to the resolution of harmonic instability in the second key area (mm. *92–109*/84–101).[62] The register of the phrase-group beginning on beat 2 of measure *92* in Version 1 is relatively undifferentiated from that in the

*Measures
92–109
84–101*

61. The elimination of the leaps within the first beat in the three lower parts of measure *91*, Version 1, also helps to make the dominant function more of a single, integrated unit of two measures: again, a macro-upbeat.

62. Though register has been shown to be problematic in numerous earlier contexts in Version 1, a somewhat elusive quality, which might be called the "center of registral gravity," claims particular attention here. With the exception of measures *86–92*, the general center of registral gravity in the second key area (and its rhyme in the recapitulation) is higher than that in the same passage in Version 2. This may in part account for some of the overall differences in the passage from measures *92* to *109*, as compared with measures *84* to *101*. In addition, the changes in part-writing establish a more compact, parallel $^6_3$ sound in measures 84–87, as compared with measures *92–95*.

Example 17

immediately preceding passage (see Exx. 15 and 17). Despite the sforzando, the continuation of the high register here fails to delineate sharply the beginning of the new phrase-group.[63] In Version 2, on the other hand, the octave drop combines with the *forte-piano* to mark clearly the beginning of the new phrase-group (beat 2, m. 84).

We can assume, since he kept it, that Beethoven wanted the high relief provided by bold registral contrast between measures *103* and *105*, Version 1/95 and 97, Version 2. Since in Version 1 he had already "used up" the high register for the first statement of the phrase-group, his choices for variety in its second occurrence (m. *100*, Version 1) were more limited than those in Version 2, where he saved the high register for the whole first part of the second phrase (mm. 92–95). His unsuccessful solution to the problem of contrast in sound in Version 1 was the octave-doubling of the top and main line (mm. *100–103*). But this posed another problem: the use of all four voices here detracts from the effect of textural intensification at the close of the passage (beginning at m. *105*/97), the passage that leads to the most decisive formal cadence for the second key area (m. *109*/101). In Version 2 the contrast and staging of the cadence (m. 101) is enhanced by the presence of only the upper three voices in measures 92–95, as well as by an augmentation of the four parts by a fifth "voice"—the double-stops in the first violin (mm. 97–100).[64]

One other consequence of the registral change for the phrase beginning at measure 84/92 can be seen in Example 18. In Version 1 the sequential patterning is broken at measure 97 (in the downward leap of a minor ninth rather than a minor second), prematurely

63. This phrase "needs" sharp delineation because it follows so immediately upon the single cadential beat (beat 1 of m. *92*) and, in a sense, before the momentum of the cadential drive begun at measure *86* has run its course.

64. The force of this cadence in Version 2 is also intensified by the rhythmic change in measure 99/*107*. The removal of the slur (cf. m. *107* to *108*, Version 1) in the upper three parts, as well as the attendant separation and sforzando of beat 3, enhances the anacrusis to the cadence at measure 101. In its heightened contrast with the *p* of measure 101, the change from the *f* (m. *108*) to *ff* (m. 100) also contributes to the dramatization of the cadence.

Example 17 (continued)

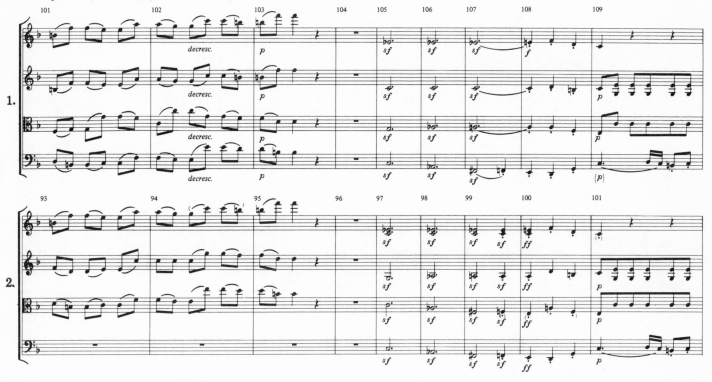

emphasizing a discontinuity created by the measure of silence (m. *96*) and the contrast in melodic figure (m. *97*, see Ex. 17). The highlighting of this disjunction in Version 1 not only weakens linear continuity within the first phrase-group (mm. *92–100*), but also ultimately detracts from the dramatic contrast (m. *105*) preceding the important cadence at measure 109. In Version 2 the modification of register (m. 84ff.) allows the patterning begun there to continue by octave replica through the entire period to measure 92 (Ex. 18). As a result, despite the break in melodic character and the four beats of silence, both of which tend to emphasize discontinuity, the turn motive is closely linked with the preceding motion (Ex. 17). Thus, registral continuity fosters greater internal coherence in the phrase-group in Version 2 by bridging a contrast in affective character. In short, the registral changes just described result in a more single motion in Version 2 (mm. 84–92). When combined with the changes in the phrase-group from measures 92 to 101 (mm. *100–109*, Version 1), they help to intensify and dramatize the most formal cadence in the second key area (m. 101/*109*).

Example 18

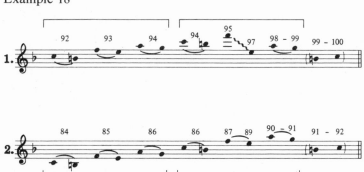

Measures
109–22
101–14

Changes in dynamics, articulation, and figuration increase stability at the end of the exposition; similarities among types of revisions emphasize differences in function.

In the final part of the closing area—the last fourteen measures in both versions—Beethoven's revisions soften the degree of articulation and produce a greater homogeneity of action in Version 2. Changes in dynamic markings, in the articulation within the viola part, and in melodic figuration all serve to increase stability.[65]

Quite typically, the revisions in dynamics are deletions: (1) the sforzando on the first beat of measures *111, 113, 115*, Version 1/103, 105, 107, Version 2; (2) the *fortissimo* at the beginning of measure *117*/109; (3) the sforzando on the second beat of measures *117–19*/109–11 (see Ex. 19).

The sforzandi in measures *111, 113*, and *115* of Version 1 only underline articulations already made clear by the syntax of other parameters. The change in harmony coincides with the two-measure grouping and is further emphasized by the internal articulation in the viola part (the motion within the first beat). In addition, the beginning of the turn motive in the cello part is synchronized with the strong beat in the other parts, particularly the strong appoggiatura figure in the first violin. The regularity of this pronounced patterning emphasizes the separation of two-measure units in Version 1. Thus, the sforzando is superfluous.

In Version 2 (mm. 101–9) Beethoven's deletion of both the sforzando and the articulation created by the skip in the viola part (m. *111ff.*/103ff., on the first beat of every

---

65. There are also changes in part-writing (mm. *116–17*/108–9), chordal stresses (mm. *117–19*/109–11), and doublings (m. *119*/111), all of which relate to the changes described in the text.

second measure) smooths out the "lumps."[66] The damping of the degree of activity in the inner parts, a kind of homogenizing of action, combines with the phrase structure to enhance stability. Appropriately for a closing area—and for the first time in the movement—the turn motive and the action of the other voices are congruent. This revision, in which the inner parts become less punctuated and more uniform, is reminiscent of the revisions made in measure 30ff. (Ex. 2).

(Indeed, the very similarity in the nature of the revisions made in these two passages, as well as in the passage at measure 72ff. (Ex. 14), suggests that Beethoven considered them to some extent comparable. Yet paradoxically, though the revisions themselves are similar, they serve to heighten differences in function.[67] Measures 29ff. and 101ff. (Exx. 2 and 19) are at once like and unlike one another. Both passages follow the most decisive formal cadences for each key area and each functions initially as a kind of "mark-time" carry-over of the momentum of arrival. But whereas the passage at measure 29ff. also functions as a preparation for departure from the first key, measure 101ff. functions, quite oppositely, to stabilize the key at the end of the exposition. The similarity between the passages also makes their differences more patent: in both, the turn motive is used as a kind of ornamental drone pedal, but in the earlier passage the revisions increase its conflict with the patterning of the first violin line; in measure 101ff., however, the revisions moderate the differences between the two outer lines and increase homogeneity.)

66. Note, however, that at the very beginning of the area of arrival, articulation within the first beat in both second violin and viola (m. *109*/101) *is* retained and helps to separate the decisive formal cadence from the ongoing motion.

67. In all three passages (mm. 29ff., 72ff., 101ff.) a variant of the opening turn motive is heard as a pedal, the inner parts are uniform and groundlike, and there is some kind of dialogue between the first violin and the cello.

Changes in figuration (in the midst of the passage, m. *113ff.*/105ff.) also contribute to a gradual weakening of the pronounced, almost martially regular procession of two-measure units in Version 1 and emphasize instead certain processive aspects of the closing area. Quite simply, in Version 2 the original turn motive, heard as a pedal point in the cello (m. 101ff.), is ornamented at measure 105 (as it was not in Version 1) so that it conforms with the impending ornamentation of the main melodic line in the first violin (m. 106);[68] this ornamentation is also reiterated in the cello part (m. 107). The resultant similarity of the cello pedal and first violin melody diminishes the degree of internal articulation created by the regular changes in harmony every two measures. The reciprocal action between these parts tends to bond them more than is possible with the maintenance of a distinct polarity of treble and bass lines, as in Version 1. In addition, the continuity of the sixteenth-note motion links these measures to those at measure 109ff. The continuity between measures 105 and 109 is strengthened by a seemingly small revision: the change in the first violin part from the appoggiatura figure of measure *113*, Version 1 to the broken-chord figure at measure 105, Version 2. The skip from C to E subtly links these measures over the musical distance. (Of course, once the cello line was changed—to begin D–C—the appoggiatura D–C in the first violin would have produced a poor harmony.) An aggregate of foreground revisions (changes in ornamentation) in Version 2 thus makes substantive differences in the coherence of the passage.

The similarity of the cello and first violin lines in Version 2 also somewhat changes the character of the passage: it now has a sing-song, almost guileless copycat quality. The conformance in figuration fuses the character of two thematic components that heretofore have been quite separate (the appoggiatura motive, as at mm. 30ff. and 43ff., and the turn motive treated as ornamental pedal point). This fusion, along with the lessening of textural polarity, subtly suggests the gradual drawing together of all action in the exposition. And this is precisely what occurs in Version 2: first a monophonic texture, beginning on the third beat of measure 109, and then a unison. All lines have, in a sense, merged as one.

In Version 1 the distinct separation of melody, pedal-ground, and accompaniment (mm. *109–16*) and the chordal accompaniment (mm. *117–19*) work against such a gradual drawing together of all action into one line. Compared with the carry-over of textural components from one phrase to the next in Version 2, the changes in Version 1 are blocked out by texture (mm. *109–16*), by the abrupt shift from *piano* to *fortissimo* (m. *117*), and by the chord disposition in the V^7–I cadence in C (mm. *116–17*). All of these underline articulation at measure *117*.

The revisions of measures *117–22*, Version 1/109–14, Version 2 resemble those from measures *86ff.*/78ff. Beethoven removes three sforzandi and two chords (on the second beat of measures) from both passages. In both cases, too, the prevailing dynamic level for the whole passage is changed from *fortissimo* in Version 1 to *piano* in Version 2 (where the *piano* dynamic has been in effect from m. 101 on). In the second passage, as in the first, this revision opens the way for the cumulative effect of a crescendo, as opposed to the block of one dynamic level jolted by sforzandi in Version 1.[69] The confusion the sforzando generates

---

68. Late eighteenth-century German theorists refer to what I am calling the main line or principal melodic action as the "Hauptstimme." See, for example, Heinrich Christoph Koch, *Musikalisches Lexikon* (Frankfurt, 1802), col. 355.

69. Indeed, it seems that at measure *117ff.* Beethoven took his cues for dynamics as well as chord placement from the passage at measure *86ff.* (see Ex. 15).

BEETHOVEN'S COMPOSITIONAL CHOICES

Example 19

in this context (m. *117ff.*) is also similar to, if not greater than, that in measure *86ff.* Melodic patterning in two-beat units is again noncongruent with the given meter and, as with the earlier passage, the sforzando transforms propulsive ambiguity into chaos (see Ex. 20).[70]

Example 20

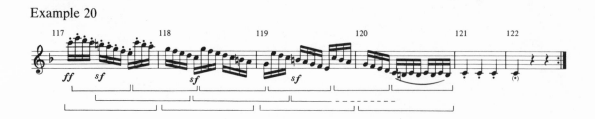

A further problem with Version 1 is the octave-doubling that begins on the last three sixteenths of measure *119* (see Ex. 19). This suggests that these notes are anacrustic to measure *120*. But a reinforced anacrusis is misplaced here for two reasons: (1) the exposition is coming to a close, and action "should be" settling down; instead, it is peculiarly propelled forward by the upbeat placement of the doubling; and (2) the harmony is all tonic here (as compared with the motion in mm. 80–81, Version 2/*88–89*, Version 1 [Ex. 15], where A can be heard as V/II moving to II in a cadential formula). The effect is one of an empty gesture of "verve," for nothing happens. In Version 2, however, the doubling occurs for the full third beat of the measure and maintains the hemiola patterning that has been ongoing from measure 109 (see beat 3, m. 111 and beat 1, m. 112).

To summarize briefly: the changes in the second key area (up to the closing area at m.*109*/101) both heighten and prolong the initial anacrustic character of the section and give greater definition and weight to its close. This is the result of the concatenation of all the revisions, especially the following: (1) the removal of one of two strong cadences that establish C at measure *72* (minor) and measure *80* (major); (2) the removal of a plateau in C minor, which is one of the chief agents of the slackening of goal-direction in Version 1; and (3) the reduction in articulation, both within and between phrases. Unlike Version 1, Version 2 maintains a tautness of line and direction in successively stronger levels, each marked by more emphatic cadences—measures 72, 84, 92, 101, and 114.[71]

70. But the confusion here (mm. *117–20*) is even more marked than in the earlier passage in Version 1 because, despite the maintenance of tonic harmony, the melodic patterning (through the C major triad) changes every two beats. That is, the patterning begins each time on a different note of the C major triad; and since the sforzandi are spaced three beats apart, in two occurrences out of three the sforzando actually coincides with the tone B rather than a tone of the C major triad. Recall that in measure *86ff.* each two-beat unit began on D and was melodically the same.

71. In the hierarchy of cadences for the second key area, measure 101 is formally the most decisive, though second in weight to that at the end of the exposition (m. 114). Not only is the hierarchy of cadences less clearly arched in Version 1, but it teeters on the edge of equalizing the cadential strength of measures *72* and *80*, as well as that of measures *92* and *100*. The only real correspondences (between versions) in cadential weight in the second key area are those at measure *109*/101 and at the end of the exposition.

3

DEVELOPMENT

THE DISCUSSION OF THE EXTENSIVE REVISIONS of the development will be divided as follows:

Measures *123–36*/115–28: up to the fugato[72]
Measures *137–56*/129–50: the fugato
Measures *157–72*/151–66: the "plateau"
Measures *173–84*/167–78: the retransition

Up to the Fugato

*Measures
123–36
115–28*

Parallelism with the beginning of the exposition is strengthened.

The revisions in the passage leading up to the fugato (Ex. 22, m. *137ff.*/129ff.)—the focal tensional event in the development—will be considered in terms of: (1) their effect on the internal structure of the passage itself; (2) the relationship of that structure to events at the beginning of the exposition; and (3) their eventual effects upon the fugato.

After the first four measures of the development,[73] the events preceding the fugato are reinterpretations of those that occurred at the beginning of the exposition, and in the very order in which they occurred there.[74] Such reinterpretation was part of a long classic tradition. Many of the changes Beethoven makes in Version 2 help to strengthen this parallelism. The relationships between the beginning of the exposition and the beginning of the development are noticeably less clear in Version 1, indeed, partly obscure. It seems

---

72. Although employed somewhat loosely, "fugato" seems the simplest and most appropriate way to refer to the imitative passage in the development.

73. The first four measures are not significantly revised.

74. Indeed, as will be shown below (p. 48 and n. 123), not only this segment but much of the development can be viewed as a reinterpretation of events of the exposition in essentially the same order in which they occurred there.

likely, on the basis of his revisions, that one of Beethoven's goals was to make these long-range connections evident. In any case, this is just what he did in Version 2.

Broadly speaking, the passage from measures *127* to *131* in Version 1 parallels that from measures *1* to *4* in the exposition, but the excessive use of the turn motive in measures *127–31* obscures the relationship (Exx. 22 and 1). In the following six measures of the development (mm. *131–37*), the connections with events of the exposition (mm. 5–8), though more tenuous, are suggested by motivic similarities.

Deletion of the turn motive and resultant registral changes affect phrase structure.

The presence of the turn motive, beginning on the same pitch, B♭, in every measure from *127* to *130*, weakens, indeed confuses, the underlying 2 + 2 grouping of measures projected by the other parts and thereby clouds the relationship of these measures to measures *1–4* in Version 1. The middle-register occurrence of the turn figure in the second violin in measures *128* and *130*, when heard in succession with measures *127* and *129*, allows only a very weak bonding of two-measure groups because the similarity of the measures precludes clear grouping.[75] Is the grouping 1 + 1 + 2 or 1 + 1 + 1 + 1 measures? Measure *128* is equivocal. The overarticulation of the passage has consequences, too, for the cumulative

75. See Cooper and Meyer, *The Rhythmic Structure of Music*, p. 85f. and pp. 139–57 *passim* for discussion of incomplete rhythms.

patterning from measures *127* to *137*, as will be shown below.

By deleting the turn motive from measures *128* and *130* in Version 1 (corresponding to mm. 120 and 122 in Version 2), Beethoven clarifies the phrase structure by making a 2 + 2 grouping of measures unequivocal in Version 2. And thus the essential line, shown in Example 21a, is heard as a correspondence with that which begins the exposition (Ex.

Example 21

21b). The damped articulation and the increased pedal-effect (on B♭) in Version 2 together dramatize the contrast between measures 119 and 123, as a group, and measures 123ff. (Ex. 22). In Version 2, measures 119–23 have more of a mark-time or "waiting" function than do the corresponding measures in Version 1 (mm. *127–31*).

A second group of revisions are registral and can be understood as consequences of the deletion of the turn motive in measures *128* and *130*. First let us consider Version 1. Use of the middle register for the turn figure at measure *131* would have seemed like a continuation of the preceding patterning; it would have created no stronger or weaker articulation than that at measures *128* and *130*. That is, by sounding the turn motive in the middle register of the second violin at measures *128* and *130*, Beethoven, in a sense, used up the possibility of its service for an articulation at measure *131*. To create that articulation, Beethoven chooses the high B♭. The octave skip also makes sense as a way of highlighting the relationship of measures *130–31* to measures *4–5* in the exposition. But the use of the high register for the turn motive at measure *131* also tends to connect it and the next measure with measure *130* rather than with what follows. Because it is a continuation of the register of the first violin in measures *128* and *130*, the high register at measure *131* detracts from the grouping of measures *131* and *132* with successive measures.[76] But since it has not been excessively employed before in Version 2, the middle register can be used for this articulation (m. *123*)—and it is Beethoven's choice. The marked registral change thus possibly helps to articulate measure 123 as a beginning of the next phase of movement. The clarity of the articulation makes the connection of measure 123 with measure 5 more palpable than it is in Version 1.

There are other immediate consequences of registral placement in Version 1. By setting the main line in the high register of the first violin at measure *131*, Beethoven leaves the ornamental figure of measure *130* melodically incomplete (the high E♭, analogous to that in measure *129*, is buried in the second violin at the lower octave, doubtless so that the turn motive on the high B♭ can begin this phase of movement).[77] Sounded over the same harmony across the bar-line, the B♭ in this register further weakens the force of the articulation at measure *131*. By comparison, the registral change at measure 123 in Version 2 allows for the completion of the ornamental figure on the first beat of measure 123 (first violin). This marks one kind of articulation, but at the same time there is no harmonic articulation. Furthermore, the choice of the high register for the first violin at measure *131* in Version 1 is partly responsible for the next problem in the segment: the disjunction in the line of tones from the B♭ (m. *131*) and C (m. *132*) to D, in the viola (m. *134*); the extreme contrast in sonority between measures *131–32* and *134*, coupled with other factors to be discussed below, contributes to disruption rather than to continuity.

An ambiguous silence is clarified by the addition of an echo.

One of the most awkward aspects of measures *132–36* in Version 1 are the silences at measures *133* and *136*, especially that at measure *133*. The silence is both jarring and confusing, partly because the registral sameness of measures *128–32*, followed by a radical break in action and sound between measures *132* and *134*, suggests that something new is about to occur. But what does occur seems at first to be some kind of response to measures *131–32*. And yet the aspect of "response" is minimized not only because of the extent to which measures *131–32* group with preceding measures, but also because measure-grouping from measure *131* is uncertain. The measure of silence is ambiguous. Is it the beginning of a new event, the end of the preceding one, or just an "in-between" measure?[78]

In Version 2 the addition of the echo at measure 125 is structurally important in both local and long-range ways. Locally, the echo delimits a pattern by making a three-measure grouping of 2 + 1 (mm. *123–25*) immediately clear, as compared with the uncertainty of grouping in the corresponding measures of Version 1. For an echo, by definition, is always an end on some hierarchic level and always relates to the event that immediately *precedes* it. The echo is important on the next level of structure as well, for the echo at measure 128 is perceived in relation to that of measure 125, as the final measure in a grouping of

$$\underbrace{\frac{2 + 1}{3}} + \underbrace{\frac{2 + 1}{3}},$$ that is, as the clear end of a pattern. Metric clarity is important

(See p. 44 for notes 76–78.)

Example 22

here because the shift from 2 + 2 (mm. 119–22) to 3 + 3 (mm. 123–28) sets up the six-measure patterning characteristic of the next section, the fugato.

Despite mobility in high-level phrase and melodic structure (to be discussed below), *two* echo phrases are as many as are likely to occur in succession in this style. Further, the echo is usually a sign of imminent change in the *type* of activity.[79] The second echo, then, is a clear sign of the end of this phase of movement and thus the articulation at measure 129 gains a clarity of function—qua beginning—not present at the analogous moment (m. *137*) in Version 1. As a sign, the echo in Version 2 becomes one agent of the dramatization of the impending fugato.

In terms of relationships over a musical distance, the echo functions in significant ways as well. Because initially one may associate the action of measures 123–24 with that of measures 5–6 of the exposition, the echo (a new gesture in the movement) is a clear break in the similarity of those two passages and signifies that the passage at measure 123ff. will not continue in the same manner as the passage at measure 5. But it is also precisely the echo that makes audible the relationship between measures 125 and 126, on the one hand, and measures 6 and 7, on the other. That is, the echo makes the line shown in Example 23a clearly analogous to the one shown in Example 23b. Thus, somewhat paradoxically perhaps, the echo at once makes the connection of the two passages clearer over the distance and functions as a sign that the passages are not the same at all![80]

Example 23

Revisions before the fugato enhance mobility.

Viewed in terms of large-scale approach to the fugato, Beethoven's revisions of measures *127–36*, Version 1/119–28, Version 2 produce harmonic differences, differences in cumulative measure- and phrase-grouping, as well as a changed main line, all of which ultimately affect the beginning of the fugato (Ex. 22). These will first be discussed as they are

76. Even if less markedly than would another reiteration of the turn motive in the middle register.

77. In a sense, the incompleteness calls attention to the figure, making the phrase at measure *131* seem to come too soon.

78. Mason, *Quartets of Beethoven*, pp. 22–23, remarks on this silent measure although he does not really analyze the problems it begets: "Common to both versions are the phrases of three measures—heavy, light, light—but in all other respects the second one immeasurably improves on the first, in which with almost childish naiveté Beethoven was still putting wrong things in right places and right things in wrong places. In the early version, the rests that fill the final measures of both phrases, making complete silences, are wrong things because, though rightly placed to give the three-measure groupings, they come upon us suddenly, without warning, and make us gasp instead of smile. Thus Beethoven, later to become a supreme master of silences as of all other dramatic effects, here bungles a silence that should stimulate our interest, turning it into a mere interruption. In the later version, he hits upon the soft echoes from the first violin that clinch his point with such indescribable charm."

79. See, for instance, the finale of Haydn's Symphony No. 100, The "Military," measures 9–12 and 13–16 in relation to measure 17ff.

80. The measure of silence in Version 1 (m. *133*) suggests that Beethoven knew that somehow he needed to break the pattern of correspondence with the passage in measures 5–8 of the exposition. But he went too far: the silence disrupts the connection, for it makes too drastic a break when combined with the registral break in the line of pitches between measures *132* and *134* (cf. mm. *6–7*).

understood in prospect; subsequently, revisions of this passage and their effect on the beginning of the fugato will be considered retrospectively, as we understand them once the fugato is under way.

One of the most fundamental changes is that of harmony and the concomitant change in the main line. In Version 1 the brief progression (B♭): IV⁶–vii–I in measures *131–34* makes the B♭ dyad (m. *134*) sound too much like a tonic for this moment in the structure. Combined with the silence and the marked registral break (between mm. *132* and *134*), the chord progression makes too emphatic an articulation. As a result, we are unsure whether measure *134* begins a new phase of movement. By comparison, the addition of G in the viola in Version 2 creates a first-inversion chord on G (m. 126), which keeps the harmony mobile. Importantly, the G_3^6 chord can be heard as part of a sequence

$$
\begin{array}{lcccc}
\text{mm. 123} & & 124\text{--}25 & 126 & 127 \\
E\flat_3^6 & & A_3^{\flat 5} & G_3^6 & C\sharp\text{----?}B\flat_3^6 \\
& & (F) & & (A)
\end{array}
$$

(Ex. 24a) in which the outer voices are clearly parallel and one-directional—parallel scales. In Version 1, on the other hand, no such sequence is evident (Ex. 24b). Because of the coherence of the harmonic sequence and the linearity of the outer voices, measures 123–29 form a single mobile segment whose process is broken only at measure 129 by the reversal of direction of the line, the effect of a deceptive cadence (d: V_7^0–VI) and the textural reduction.

Example 24

In terms of the main line of action, too, the D in the viola (m. *134*) in Version 1 is at best a disjunct continuation of the line B♭–C begun in the first violin at measure *131* (Ex. 22). Coupled with the harmonic motion, its contrast in sonority and register with the preceding part of the main line seems to suggest that this may be a beginning. In measure *135*, the second violin is heard as a kind of "answer" to the "subject" in the viola in measure *134*. This not only obscures the completion of the viola gesture (the descending major sixth) as a parallel construction to measures *131–33*, but it also suggests that a fugal passage may have been ongoing and that somehow we may have missed its beginning![81]

One result of the organization of measures *127–37* in Version 1 is that the grouping from measure *127*

$$
\left(\underbrace{\frac{1+1}{?}+\frac{1+1}{?}}_{?}+\frac{2+1}{3?}? +\frac{\overline{1+1}+1}{3?}\right)
$$

is additive and unclear; for this reason, it has little drive to the next important articulation (m. *137*). On the other hand, the grouping from measure 119 of Version 2

$$
\left(\underbrace{2+2}+\frac{2+1}{3}+\frac{2+1}{3}\right)
$$

is cumulative and goal-directed (toward m. 129).

81. In addition, of course, the dissonance of the viola's G against the G♯ and A on the third beat in the second violin is very problematic.

Other aspects of the revisions already mentioned, as well as revisions not yet considered, can best be understood retrospectively, that is, in relation to the beginning of the fugato. To facilitate discussion of these matters, the beginning of the fugato will be considered cursorily here, with the main discussion of the fugato below (pp. 47–61).

The beginning of the fugato becomes more palpable.

If any one factor can be singled out as undercutting the force of the beginning of the fugato in Version 1, it is this: melodically measure *134* exactly prefigures the opening measure (m. *137*), albeit over the tone B♭ (Ex. 25). As already suggested, measure *134* itself sounds like a beginning, an aspect that is underscored when it is followed immediately (m. *135*) by an "answer" at the fifth above. Because of the prominence of the second violin, combined with the prominence and "beginning" aspects of measure *134*, it is not at all clear that measure *135* is the end of anything.[82] The parallelism of measures *132* and *135* is lost, or at least submerged: we do not know whether measure *135* is a middle or an end. Thus, instead of being a bold articulation, measure *137* (the "true" beginning of the fugato) sounds like a return to the kind of action heard at measure *134*. There is gestural confusion.

Example 25

There is harmonic confusion in Version 1 as well. The beginning of the fugato helps to account for the harmonic revisions Beethoven makes in the passage from measures *132* to *137*, Version 1/124 to 129, Version 2. Even without the benefit of our knowledge of Version 2, it is clear that in both versions D major or minor has been a harmonic target from the first four measures of the development. The motion to B♭ at measure *127*/119 sounds like a deceptive cadence (Ex. 22). In Version 1, however, the harmonic route to D/d becomes unclear when the diminished triad on A (m. *132*) moves to the dyad B♭–D: the effect is that of a V–I cadence in B♭, albeit weak by virtue of the voice-leading (Ex. 25). More problematic still is the strong V^6_5 of D/d (m. *135*) that moves (m. *137*) to a fleeting resolution on D. By beat 2 of measure *138* we know the key is G minor and *not* D minor. The resolution is a kind of sham,[83] and as a result there is not an adequate amount of D minor in Version 1.[84]

In Version 2, contrastingly, the sequence beginning at measure 123 generates mobility and goal-directedness; the increased regularity of this sequence also heightens the motion to

82. Because of its registral position, the second violin part (m. *135*), as noted earlier, tends to dominate the measure and to weaken the audibility of the descending major sixth in the viola. This sixth parallels that in measure *132*, which was retrospectively understood as an end of a phrase.

83. It works partly because the motion toward D minor had been de-intensified by the deflection to B♭ at measure *134*. The original harmonic trajectory (to D/d) had lost force enroute to measure *135*, taken on quite specific implications at measure *135*, and then realized those implications incompletely at measure *137* because of the quick twist from D to G, as the tonic of the ensuing passage (mm. *137–42*). G minor may ultimately be understood simply as the relative minor of B♭. The premature appearance of the "subject" on D (m. *134*) is first heard as the third in B♭ and then, in the fugato proper, as the fifth in G.

84. This is partly because Beethoven "used up" the B♭ in Version 1 too soon (m. *134*).

Bb (m. 129) and simultaneously makes it a point of articulation (Ex. 26a).[85] Had the sequence continued regularly, it would have moved through C (m. 127) to D (m. 129) as the bass of a Bb$_3^6$ chord (Ex. 26b). The Bb is marked for attention both because the line is reversed with this pitch and because it functions as a deceptive cadence in D minor.

Example 26

The Bb at measure 129, then, serves two immediate functions: (1) it underscores this moment as an important articulation of the structure precisely because it is *not* the expected tone, and (2) it allows Beethoven to write the beginning of the fugato in the key of D minor, the key, that has, after all, been indicated as a harmonic goal since the first four measures of the development. Beethoven has made the entire passage from measure 119 clearer and more regular, so that the one deflection of the implied motion (m. 129, a kind of "checkpoint" moment in regular phrase-grouping) is more forceful than the longer deflection in measures *134–35* of Version 1 (in Ex. 22).

In addition, the revisions in Version 2 establish clearer relationships over a distance. The motion to the Bb in the cello at measure 129—at a crucial *juncture* in the development— is heard as a deceptive cadence, just as it was at measure 119; as a result, the relationship between measures 119 and 129 is evident. For this reason, too, the whole passage from measure 119 to 129 can, in one sense, be understood as parenthetical or, in any case, as a way of delaying the central event of the development, the fugato. These are decisive moments in the large-scale articulation of the structure. By contrast, measure *127* in Version 1 is partly analogous to measure *134*, but the Bb is heard as bVI in measure *127* whereas it is tonicized at measure *134*.[86]

The Fugato

Large-scale harmonic revisions relate the fugato both to immediately preceding events and to the opening of the movement.

Measures 137–56 129–50

The changes in the fugato (mm. *137–56/129–50*) are the most considerable in the entire movement. Because so many revisions occur and because these interact in complex ways, the discussion of this segment will be organized first according to temporal order in the movement and within formal segments, and then according to equivalent tonal areas.

85. Peter Gram Swing called my attention to a linear connection between the passage immediately preceding the fugato and the very beginning of the fugato. It is the line formed by E–G (second violin and its echo in the first violin) just preceding the fugato in Version 2 and Bb–C# at the beginning of the fugato (cello). The tones E–G–Bb–C# form the very diminished seventh chord on C# that finally resolves at measures 133–34 in the fugato. This line straddles—indeed, moves through—the articulation on Bb.

86. The Bb at measure 129 of Version 2 also links this moment and that at measure 119 with measure 151—as focal articulations in the development.

The most striking revisions are in the harmonic plan, in the thoroughgoing intensification and integration of rhythmic activity, and in the lengthening of Version 2 by two measures. Practically all of the other revisions may be linked to these.

The harmonic sequence that moves to B♭ minor at measure *157/151*—clearly the next big junction in the movement in *both* versions—is changed as follows (also see Ex. 28):

	mm.	*137*	*143*	*149*	*155*	
Version 1:		G minor	C minor	F minor	B♭ minor	
		6 mm.	6 mm.	6 mm.	2 mm.	

	mm.	129	135	141	147	149
Version 2:		D minor	G minor	C minor	F minor	B♭ minor
		6 mm.	6 mm.	6 mm.	2 mm.	2 mm.

As mentioned earlier, G minor, the harmonic point of departure for the fugato in Version 1, is an evasion of the originally implied course toward D. D minor, as VI in F, is one conventional turning point in the harmonic path back to the tonic. Perhaps that is one reason Beethoven chose D minor, not G minor, for the beginning of the fugato in Version 2. But there are other possible explanations.

One striking possibility is that Beethoven wanted to continue the succession of connections between the events at the beginning of the exposition and those following the fourth measure of the development (see pp. 39, 44).[87] For the sequence of diminished sevenths that informs the passage beginning at measure 13 is the very one that spells out the harmonic revision of the fugato in Version 2—namely, diminished sevenths on C♯ (for D minor) in measures 14 and 130f.; on F♯ (for G minor) in measures 16 and 136f.; and, though separated in time in the exposition, perhaps even the one on B (for C minor) in measures 22 and 142f. (Ex. 27).[88]

Because of these relationships over a distance and because the revised key succession is, significantly, centered on the revised succession of diminished sevenths, it is not likely that it was merely the characteristic sonority of the diminished seventh that Beethoven cared about here.[89] Indeed, as can be seen in Examples 27a and 27b (with the restatement of mm. 1–4 omitted), measures 13–14 and 129–30 correspond, and (with mm. 131–34, which prolong VII, omitted) measures 15–16 and 135–36 correspond. (A case might also be made for the correspondence of measures 21–22 and measures 141–42.)

In Version 1 the succession of diminished sevenths in the fugato corresponds at the interval of a fifth below to that in the passage from measure *13* in the exposition. But the di-

87. Of course, in Version 1 the transposition down a fifth (beginning on B♭ in the development) from the exposition in one sense maintains a more exact parallelism than is present in Version 2. But this unbroken parallelism is less tensional than the deflection in Version 2, which makes clear both the parenthetical aspect of B♭ (see p. 47) and the associated relationship of A (as V), at the very beginning of the development, to D minor at the beginning of the fugato.

88. Indeed, each successive six-measure segment of the fugato in Version 2 might be regarded as an exploration of each of the diminished sevenths in the first key area of the exposition, beginning at measure 13.

It is possible that one might extend the line of harmonic correspondence to measure 24 (corresponding to mm. 147–48) and measure 26 (corresponding to m. 149 *if* D♭ in m. 147 is reinterpreted as C♯, with C♯ being the root of a diminished seventh for D in the exposition and D♭ the diminished seventh of the chord on E at m. 147). The functions of measures 24 and 147–48 are surely *not* analogous but the chord succession in the exposition may have continued to be suggestive. All of this is perhaps more convincing when the next, and closer, correspondence is noted: the dominant seventh of B♭ (m. 26) in the exposition corresponds to the diminished seventh chord on A (dominant function in B♭ minor, m. 149) in the development.

An association of textures over the musical distance also supports the parallelism in Version 2: the first solo presentation of the turn motive in the exposition is at measure 13 and the first solo presentation of the turn motive in the development is at the beginning of the fugato, measure 129. This association is not clear in Version 1 because both measures *5 and 13* are soloistic.

89. Kerman writes: "he [Beethoven] cared not about the specific harmonic function of the diminished-7ths, but about their characteristic sonority per se" (*Beethoven Quartets*, p. 33).

Example 27

minished seventh is completely missing as the characteristic sonority in the first four measures of the fugato (Ex. 28, m. *137ff.*). Instead, the less tensional interval of the minor sixth is heard in the place where the diminished seventh later takes over.[90] The intensity provided by the diminished seventh at the very beginning of the revised version of the fugato is symptomatic of the comprehensive intensification of action in the fugato of Version 2. This will be discussed as follows: (1) six-measure segments from both versions in the temporal order in which they occur (despite differences in key) and (2) passages from each version that are comparable because they are in the same key.

At the very beginning of the fugato in Version 1, an almost martially regular procession of one-measure units troops by in registral order from low to high (Ex. 28). In Version 2, by contrast, a stretto effect at measure 131 heightens tension by counteracting regularity.[91] In addition to local reasons for this revision,[92] the reposeful regularity of blocked measure-to-measure action in the impending sixteen-measure "plateau" (beginning at m. *157/151*) would have been undercut at least partly by the similar measure-to-measure action in the fugato of Version 1. In short, if the regularity characteristic of the next big phase of movement is to be effective, the fugato must contrast with it; it must create tension.

Contrapuntal revisions **within** *six-measure segments, combined with changes in dynamics, increase intensity and coherence; melodic (registral) changes articulate division between segments.*

The rhythmic integration that Beethoven effects by his revision within six-measure units of the fugato will be considered after the first segment of Version 1 has been discussed. The internal formal structure of this first segment will be analyzed both for itself and as an exemplar of what happens in each of the six-measure segments in this version. The sameness of the first four measures of Version 1, except for registral and timbral differences, results in a $\dfrac{4}{1 + 1 + 1 + 1}$ measure-grouping (Ex. 28). The regularity of

90. This, of course, establishes a nonuniformity in the overall construction of successive groups of six measures, that is, between mini-expositions. The absence of the diminished seventh in this phase of the fugato in Version 1 may have been one influence on Beethoven's revised succession of temporary tonal centers—to include D minor at the beginning of the harmonic sequence.

91. Though in the present context irregularity heightens tension, I do not mean to imply that there is any inherent or universal connection between irregularity and tension. And rhythmic regularity can, of course, be tensional, for instance, in ostinatos heard over a dominant pedal just before a recapitulation, or in a sequence that is harmonically goal-directed (as in a transition or a development). See, for example, measures 96–109 of the first movement of Beethoven's "Waldstein" Sonata.

92. One of the casualties of the insistent regularity of the procession from cello to the first violin in Version 1 is that of part-writing: the line F♯–G–G♯ in measure *139* is scattered from viola to cello and results in a lack of linear clarity. In the G minor passage of Version 2, Beethoven saves the cello entrance so that the motion from F♯ through to C can be heard as a single line (mm. 137–39).

---

registral order emphasizes the completion of one cycle of entrances by all members of the quartet. Since each instrument has had its turn, so to speak, the fourth entrance by the first violin, as the last member of this cycle, is a kind of minimal sign that one phase of movement has ended and a new sort of action is imminent.[93]

The signaled change occurs "on schedule" at the beginning of measure *141*. It is emphasized by the sforzando in the three lowest parts on the first beat of the measure, by the skip in the first violin from D (m. *140*) down to F♯ (m. *141*), by the introduction of the diminished seventh chord for the first time in this segment, and by the new patterning within measure *141*. The first violin's completion of a pattern at the end of measure *140* takes precedence over the tendency of the last two beats in the three lower parts (in rhythmic unison) to group across the bar-line with measure *141*.[94] Thus, the potential six-measure phrase is not strongly delimited as such;[95] rather, it is divided as follows:

$$\text{m. }137 \qquad\qquad 141$$
$$\underbrace{1 + 1 + 1 + 1}_{4?} + \underbrace{1 + 1}_{2?}.$$

The overall grouping of measures *137–42* in Version 1 is additive rather than cumulative; the measures are weakly bonded except for key.

In Version 2 the stretto-like fourth entrance of the turn motive (m. 131) is one of the decisive elements in the integration within six-measure segments of the fugato. As a break in the measure-by-measure succession of regular imitative entries, the stretto welds the action between the third and the fourth measures (mm. 131–32) of the six-measure unit. The rhythmic position of the fourth entrance (second violin) of the "subject" allows the statement of the turn motive to be completed on beat 1 of measure 132, thus freeing the second and third beats of measure 132 for the marked break in process that occurs. (In other words, had the fourth entrance been regular, as in Version 1, the second and third beats would have presented the end of the turn motive.) The new position of the fourth entrance also functions as a sign that the basic type of action is about to change.

In the revision, too, the marked break in process—in motive, line, and texture—that occurs after the first beat of measure 132 creates a strong impulse toward measure 133. One result is a clear two-beat anacrusis to the beginning of measure 133. At the same time, and particularly after measure 134 is heard, measure 133 is understood as the beginning of a pattern, as well as the point of arrival for a grouping begun on beat 2, measure 132. In sum, an overlap binds the action of the first four measures to that of the last two in the six-measure segment. This may be shown as

The revised placement of the sforzandi also promotes rhythmic integration and increases the energy at the ends of each segment of the fugato. In Version 1 the first violin's sforzando occurs on the second beat of the measure (mm. *141–42* and *147–48*), as in Version 2. But unlike Version 2, the sforzandi in the three lowest parts are on the first beat. By assimilating beats 2 and 3 as almost inconsequential afterbeats, these first-beat stresses tend to emphasize the measure as a unit and to weaken the forward motion.[96] In Version 2 the coincidence of sforzandi on the second beat of the measure in all four parts energizes the measure internally. The instability created by this offbeat stress prevents the squareness characteristic of Version 1. The sforzandi in this position create an effect analogous both to the stretto entrance of the fourth voice of the fugato (m. 131, second violin) and to the emphasis created by the disjunction in measure 132, beat 2. This effect not only links the "tail" to the preceding four measures, but also suggests motion across the bar-line (that is,

(See p. 53 for notes 93–96.)

Example 28

as in the stretto moving from m. 131 to m. 132 and the first violin, m. 132, beat 2, moving to m. 133).

What immediately follows the first six-measure segments in each version also influences the integration within those segments. In Version 1 the registral placement (first violin) of the beginning of the second six-measure group creates a linear continuity (F#–G–A♭) from measure *142* to *143*. This further undermines the formal integrity of the first six-measure group. For, despite the change in key and the reduction of the texture to a single line at measure *143*—both signs that a new segment is beginning—the A♭ (m. *143*) may be heard not as a new beginning but as a linear continuation of the preceding phrase. The result is an ambiguity of phrase structure. (This is discussed below.) In Version 2, by comparison, the second segment, beginning in measure 135, is clearly separated from what precedes it. This is so not only because of the registral disjunction and the change in harmony and texture, but also because the first segment is itself internally coherent.

The revisions of rhythmic integration in the second and third six-measure segments of the fugato are similar to those of the first. But the characteristics retained, as well as the changes in part-writing, suggest that Beethoven, at least partly, may have used key areas rather than just the succession of segments as the basis for some of his revisions.[97] For this reason, and particularly since revisions of part-writing are more readily apparent in the *same* key, equivalent tonal areas will be compared. (The last two measures of each six-measure segment, which I call the "tails," are of particular interest.)[98] The part-writing and its effect on the articulation of structure will be discussed in the order of segments: G minor, C minor, and F minor (Ex. 29).

93. The signs in Version 2 are much clearer (see below). One might also consider the slight modification of the turn figure itself (E♭ instead of E♮) as it occurs the fourth time in the first violin, a subtle hint of change.

94. The separation between measures *140* and *141* is, however, not unmitigated. Partly because of the disposition of the parts, the chromatic chain of parallel $^6_3$'s that moves upward under the turn motive in the first violin (m. *140*) is heard separately from the main line of the "subject." The smooth progression of the $^6_3$'s tends to carry the motion across the bar-line.

95. On the one hand, measures *141–42*, taken together, form a unit separated from the preceding measures by virtue of their difference from those; on the other hand, these measures do not bond internally precisely because they are identical. For a discussion of the relationship between repetition and the separation of events, see Meyer, *Explaining Music*, pp. 50–53.

96. This is particularly the case in measures *141–42*, as opposed to the ends of later six-measure segments, because of the ♩♩♪ pattern. However, even in measures *147–48*, *153–54*, and *155–56*, the blocked-measure effect remains.

97. On the other hand, the last two measures of each segment, taken in chronological order, are rhythmically similar, thus suggesting that rhythm at the ends of six-measure segments may have guided Beethoven's revisions.

98. Interestingly, the sketches to the revision of the fugato (see n. 12) are focused on the "tails." Indeed, Beethoven has, for the most part, sketched "tails" contiguously! Of thirteen measures of sketches for the revision of this passage, eight are for the "tails."

Details of part-writing in equivalent tonal areas affect structure and continuity.

The G minor segments (mm. *137–42*/135–40): in Version 2 the pairing of voices in thirds (mm. 139–40), with the pairs registrally well separated, is combined with the motion of the highest line from A to B♭ (rather than from F♯ to G, as in Version 1, mm. *141–42*); this has two effects. First, the main line in the first violin is more mobile because the third instead of the tonic is uppermost and because the third, rather than the root, is doubled in the G minor chord. Second, the disposition of the diminished seventh chord in Version 2 is more biting and edgy than its more evenly spaced counterpart in Version 1; the placement of the E♭ and F♯ between viola and second violin in Version 2 intensifies the instability of the chord (mm. 139–40).

As suggested above, the disposition of the voices in Version 1 ultimately detracts from the clarity of articulation of the subsequent segment in C minor. On the one hand, the motion from F♯ to G has apparently closed the G minor segment. Yet at the next moment one is in doubt because the motion to A♭ in the same voice establishes its own strong continuity. In Version 2 the motion from A to B♭ in the first violin is more mobile despite the fact that the six-measure unit is itself more integrated and better delimited by internal means (though *not* closed). The openness of the main line in Version 2 does not interfere with the clarity of definition of the G minor segment qua segment.

Further, the change in instrumentation—to the viola (m. 141)—in Version 2 provides a marked contrast in timbre and sonority with the end of the first six measures. Together with the reversal of direction in the main line (A–B♭, m. 140, to A♭, m. 141), this contrast makes clear that measure 141 is a beginning.[99] In short, the open end of the main line in the first violin (mm. 139–40) impels the fugato without marring clarity of structure. The closed end of the line in Version 1 does not even adequately delimit the end of the segment because the line is abruptly and confusingly reopened.[100]

The C minor segments (mm. *143–148*/141–46): here, too, small changes in part-writing make important differences. In Version 1 (m. *144ff*.) the first violin line is once again problematic because its registral prominence and goal-directed chromatic ascent tend to obscure the fourth imitative entrance of the turn motive in the second violin (m. *146*). Further, after the stepwise ascent, the reiteration of F in the first violin (m. *146*) suggests a break in the preceding process; but then, as another case of "misplaced continuity," the F regains its upward ascent, thus clouding the division between measures *146* and *147*.

The voice-leading in this C minor segment of Version 1 is particularly poor: specifically, the parallel octaves on the last beat (A♭–G) in measures *147* and *148*, and the weak resolution of the prominent leading tone, B, in the second violin to C in the *viola* at the end of the third beat in the measure.[101] In the revisions of the C minor passage in Version 2, the part-writing is improved. The clearer voice-leading highlights the leading-tone drive in C minor. First, the tone B (mm. 145–46) moves to C in the *same* voice, the second violin. Second, in its disposition between the two violins, the instability of the vertical interval of the diminished seventh is specially intense (m. 145). Thus, unlike its corresponding moment in Version 1 (m. *147*, beat 1), measure 145 does not relax the harmonic tension created by the strong leading-tone drive in measure 144ff. In fact, the leading-tone drive itself is emphasized by the leap of the minor seventh in the first violin (m. 144), the approach to B in the second violin (end of m. 144, beginning of m. 145), and the smooth resolution of the seventh to a perfect fifth (beat 1 to beat 3 in mm. 145 and 146).[102]

The F minor segments (mm. *149–54*/147–48): in Version 1 the F minor segment is, of course, a full six-measure segment of the fugato; in Version 2 it is just a two-measure segment where, in a sense, the two measures now serve as surrogate for six (see discussion

(See pp. 56, 57 for notes 99–102.)

Example 29

below on rhythmic revisions). Briefly, the *lines* at measures *153–54* in Version 1 are revised in Version 2 so that the cello's line (but not its rhythm) is heard in the first violin (mm. *147–48*). The leading tone, E, set more than two octaves above the B♭–D (in second violin and viola), is acutely unstable. Even the sudden absence of the cello in these two measures accentuates the instability, as well as the basic change in action, that occurs here. The change in texture and the small modification in rhythm, as compared with the two preceding measures, are part of a set of signs that the "expositions" are over. One other result of the revised part-writing here is that the $\frac{6}{3}$ position of the tonic harmony is maintained at the ends of all the "tails" and contributes to the form of the passage.[103]

The revised part-writing, especially in the "tails" within the fugato, also influences the clarity of rhythmic counterpoint in the passage. In Version 1 the part-writing muddies the distinction between the two patterns ♫♩♪ and ♩♫♫ ; that is, these patterns are not kept clearly separated as strands of the texture (Ex. 29). For example, in measures *153–54* the rhythms of the cello and second violin pair against those of the first violin and viola; but the viola is set so far below the first violin, and so close to the cello and second violin, that its rhythm tends to blend with and confuse the lower parts rather than to join with the first violin. In Version 2, however, the part-writing in each two-measure "tail" coordinates with the rhythmic counterpoint.[104] There is similar coordination in the "tails" of the C minor segment (with the three lower parts in rhythmic unison against the top voice) and the F minor segment.

In revising part-writing in the fugato, Beethoven established several kinds of linear connections *between* segments, connections that enhance continuity through the fugato. The changes in line complement those in part-writing and vice versa.[105] Both the revised cello and first violin lines of each of the "tails" intensify directionality and connections between segments. The revised cello line (mm. 133 and 134, 139 and 140) leads linearly to the pitch that begins the next segment of the fugato (Ex. 30). In each case, registral displacement for the first subject entrance not only helps to articulate the beginning of the segment, but also, by being "deceptive" registrally, it calls attention to the implicit linear continuity.[106]

99. Still another possible reason for the revision of measures *141–42* is that, when heard retrospectively in relation to the next two-measure "tail" (mm. *147–48*), the F♯–G followed by A♭–G (mm. *147–48*) in the highest line seems a bit circular.

100. From the point of view of successive passages, one of the similarities between third segments in both versions is that each begins in the viola.

101. The motion on the first two beats in the second violin is also problematic from the standpoint of correct intonation by the performer.

Example 30

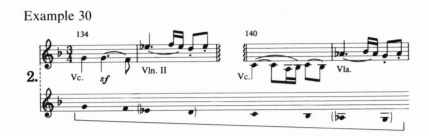

Appropriately, this particular continuity of line is severed at the end of the C minor segment in Version 2 (that is, mm. 145–46 do not lead to mm. 147–48 in the manner shown in Ex. 30) precisely where the fugato proper (the three six-measure mini-expositions) is broken (Ex.

102. Indeed, Beethoven may have moved the line to A♭ on beat 2 in measure 144 rather than F—which would have been the tone if either the correspondence with measure 138, Version 2 or that with measure *146*, Version 1 were maintained—in order to ensure the presence of the sound of the diminished seventh on the first beat here in Version 2. The motion to A♭ in the first violin also puts the cello in the position to play the line that the first violin would otherwise have had.

103. Moreover, had the cello line of measure 146 (cf. m. *148*, Version 1) continued as in measure *153*, Version 1 (cello), the outer voices in Version 2 would have been in parallel diminished fifths, as well as sequential in a stepwise manner—scarcely a way of highlighting the break with the main part of the fugato!

104. The sketches for the revision of the "tails" of the G and C minor segments are closer to their final realization in Version 2 than are those for the D minor segment. (Of course, D minor was apparently the last tonal center Beethoven settled upon.) In these sketches, one sees Beethoven laboring over the coordination of part-writing and rhythmic counterpoint.

105. It would be interesting to know the order of changes—whether Beethoven first worked at the linear connections, which then affected the part-writing, or vice versa. Of course, the revisions may have been conceived for the simultaneous improvement of both.

106. In each segment there is also a linear and registral continuity between the stretto (or fourth) occurrence of the turn motive and the "tail," which then connects with the following stretto entrance. Thus: B♭–A (first violin, mm. 131–32), G–F (cello, mm. 133–34), E♭–D (viola, mm. 137–38), C–B♭ (cello, mm. 139–40), A♭–G, displaced up one octave (second violin, mm. 143–44). This is shown in the example below:

28). In Version 1 this reversal of the same pattern occurs very much *in medias res*, at the end of the second segment (mm. *147–48*).

Another kind of continuity that affects, and is affected by, the changed part-writing in Version 2 is evident in the highest line at the ends of each segment of the fugato. The descending sequential pattern from the high E (beat 2, m. 132) down to the G on the last eighth-note in measure 146 (see Ex. 31) shapes this other aspect of continuity through the fugato. The break in this patterning, with the reiteration of A♭ (beat 3, m. 144) rather than immediate continuation to G, and the descent to G (mm. 145–46),[107] signals the impending break in the imitative entries of the fugato (m. 147).[108] The descent here, which is followed not by a continuation to the implied F but by a bold silence in the first violin (beat 1, m. 147), contributes to the precipitous character of measures 147–48.

Example 31

Rhythmic revisions intensify drive and set the stage for the next phase of movement.

The urgent character of the two-measure segment in F minor in Version 2—and, as the movement continues, the entire six measures from 145 to 151—has a great deal to do with

107. The approach from above, rather than from below, as in the analogous moments of the preceding two segments, emphasizes this change.

108. This break is also complemented by the break mentioned in the previous paragraph and in n. 107.

rhythmic revisions at the end of the fugato (Ex. 32). As suggested above, rhythmic revisions in the measures before the "plateau" can be understood partly in the light of the upcoming "plateau," since the relaxation provided by the latter depends to a large extent on the tension that precedes it. The role of two additional measures in Version 2 (mm. 149–50) is, of course, intricately linked with the total revision, but for the immediate discussion their presence will simply be assumed. Their important role in both the process and the form of the development will be taken up separately.

The lack of clarity in the rhythmic counterpoint of measures *153–54* in Version 1 has already been mentioned. In the next two measures (*155–56*) rhythmic counterpoint is clear. However, these two measures create new rhythmic problems. They neither continue the patterning of the preceding two measures nor lead to the beginning of the "plateau" at measure *157*. Rather, they relate back to the "tails" of the first two six-measure segments (Ex. 28). The alternation of patternings in two-measure groups (particularly if one includes the beginning of the "plateau" at m. *157*) is somewhat confusing. It not only tends to demand attention in itself, but also detracts from the drive toward the "plateau" and creates a rhythmically abrupt transition to it.

In Version 2 the reversal of the arrangement of rhythms in the "tails" of the first two segments, ♫♩ ♪ (mm. 133–34, 139–40) to ♩ ♫♫ (mm. 145–46), is essentially maintained in the two successive two-measure units (mm. 147–48, mm. 149–50)[109] as well as

109. As suggested above, p. 56, the clarity of the separate rhythmic strands in this version is greatly enhanced by the revised part-writing. This rearrangement, of course, occurs in both versions at corresponding measures in the fugato (mm. *153–54*, Version 1/mm. *145–46*, Version 2). In Version 2 it functions as one of a set of signs that the fugato will no longer continue imitatively. Note, in this regard, that at measure 147 Beethoven avoids the original rhythm of the "subject," the measure that would have initiated the next mini-exposition, had there been one. In Version 1 the "sign" is confusing in retrospect because it is immediately contradicted by a return to earlier patterning (that at mm. *141–42* and *147–48*).

for the beginning of the "plateau" (m. 151f.; see Ex. 32a). This similarity in rhythmic construction between measures 145–46 and 147–48 has several noteworthy consequences. One is immediate: the sudden truncation (absence of sound in the first violin) on beat 1, measure 147, is propulsive and urgent partly because the very likeness of the two-measure groups in succession makes us attend to the small but significant difference. More importantly, the similarity in grouping and in internal rhythmic construction focuses attention on an effect of compression: it is as if the previous six-measure units are now all jammed together into just their goals (Ex. 32a and 28). There is an effect of stretto, both because of the quick succession of "tails" and because the truncation (mm. 147–48) and the change in texture highlight the imitation of the motive ♪♫ at the distance of one beat. (This has been the case throughout in the close of each six-measure segment, but the revisions here tend to spotlight it.) The similarity in rhythmic patterning in the three groups of two-measure units directs attention to the drive toward the next phase of movement, the "plateau." And this drive is of course related to the addition of two measures at the end of the fugato in Version 2.

The two added measures in the fugato of Version 2 (mm. 147–48)[110] constitute a typically small change with notable consequences for coherence.[111] Because of rhythmic similarities, as well as the regular schedule of changes in temporary tonal centers—the end of the C minor segment, the two measures each of F minor and B♭ minor—the final three

two-measure units may be understood as $\overbrace{2 + \underbrace{2 + 2}_{4}}^{6}$. The composite structural length

makes possible the smooth continuity from the basic six-measure module of action in the main part of the fugato to the four-measure module of the upcoming "plateau." But at the same time the C minor segment (mm. 145–46) is also heard *as* an end; it relates to the other two-measure units (in D minor and G minor) that ended the mini-expositions. Both for this reason and because of the change in the nature of the action at measures 147–48, the F minor segment also begins a group and is a signal for the larger change that is imminent. Because of its length and activity, the B♭ minor segment then groups with the F minor segment. The four-measure grouping paves the way for the structural lengths of the next segment (m. 151ff.).

The subtly dovetailed shift in unit lengths and the concomitant change in the durations of temporary tonal centers (from six to two measures), combined with the rhythmic stretto, intensify instability and propel motion forward. Paradoxically, because the impression is one of "ends" all in a row, the mounting rhythmic tension of the 2 + 2 measure segment (mm. 147–50) acts as a large anacrusis to the "plateau" and release that follow. In Version 1, on the other hand, the passage moves forward only weakly. Because the measures are grouped $(\underline{4 + \underline{2} + 2})$ so that a long unit (mm. *149–52*) is followed by shorter ones that seem like afterbeats (mm. *153–54, 155–56*), this passage lacks anacrustic character and

110. However, both versions have a two-measure group in B♭ minor, each one differing mainly in the arrangement of its rhythms. Since this two-measure group is, in one sense, a constant, Beethoven may have used it as a point of departure for prior revisions. It would seem that, since he wanted only two measures in F minor (mm. 147–48) in Version 2 (cf. six measures in Version 1, mm. *149–54*), he found that one way to achieve the two-measure unit in Version 2 was to begin the circle of fifths of the fugato one cycle earlier—D minor rather than G minor (as in Version 1). Needless to say, he might have revised Version 1 in such a way that F minor would have come in the position it did, but only for two measures. However, this would have disrupted the extent of the mini-expositions (i.e., there would not have been three full ones).

111. These two measures will eventually be related to parallels in proportions between the exposition and the development. See n. 123.

Example 32

thrust (Ex. 32b). Further, it fails to connect with the preceding structural lengths of six measures each. Neither the retrospective nor prospective links in structural lengths exist in Version 1 where the F minor passage is followed by only two measures in B♭ minor.

After so much change, the relatively minimal revision of the two measures in B♭ minor at the end of the fugato (mm. 149–50/*155–56*) is noteworthy (Ex. 32a and b). As has been mentioned, only the arrangement of rhythms within measures was revised. The changed placement of the sforzando in measures 149–50 (versus mm. *155–56*) is more propulsive and ultimately helps to delineate the change in character between the end of the fugato and the beginning of the ''plateau.'' Not only does the revised rhythm in Version 2 establish retrospective connections (with mm. 145–46 and 147–48), but it works together with the absence of harmonic change between this passage and the beginning of the next (m. 151). This results in a uniformity that directs attention to the release from the preceding textural tug-of-war—a wholly new affect. The rhythm of the first violin, as well as the harmony across the bar-line, remains constant at the juncture in Version 2 (end of m. 150; beginning of m. 151), and this constancy highlights the contrast. In Version 1, on the other hand, the listener must attend once more to a shift in the rhythm of the principal line.[112] This detracts from the effect of immediate calm at the beginning of the ''plateau'' (m. *157*).

112. See Meyer, *Explaining Music*, p. 54, for a theory that supports this point.

The "Plateau"[113]

Measures
157–72
151–66

Revisions of harmonic plan, texture, instrumentation, and rhythm heighten affect and strengthen coherence.

Occurring as it does between two passages of high intensity—one the fugato, the other the immediate preparation for the recapitulation—the sixteen-measure passage beginning at measure *157*/151 functions as a relatively quiet plateau. However, this character and function are only partially realized in Version 1. Beethoven's revisions heighten the affective quality, promote internal coherence, and intensify structural bonding. The main revisions involve the harmonic plan, texture and instrumentation, and groupings of measures and phrases.

On the basis of what is retained from Version 1, we may infer that Beethoven was concerned with uniformity and regularity in this passage (Ex. 33). In both versions the basic texture is melody and accompaniment;[114] and the motion is blocked out in four-measure harmonic units, where the main line in each unit takes the turn motive, measure by measure,

113. The designation of this segment as a "plateau" is of course metaphorical; hereafter, the word will be used without quotation marks.

114. Textural changes within this basic framework will be shown to figure importantly; see below, pp. 65–66.

through one arpeggio.[115] In his revised version, Beethoven went considerably further in the direction of uniformity and regularity; he made the music more placid. The streamlined version is both more internally coherent and more tightly integrated with the immediate retransition (see discussion below). The harmonic arc of action to the dominant pedal preparation is one of the most salient revisions.

The harmonic plan of the plateau was changed as follows:

		157–60	*161–64*	*165–68*	*169–72*
Version 1:	mm.	b♭	G♭	C(V) →	f

		151–54	155–58	159–62	163–66
Version 2:	mm.	b♭	G♭	f	D♭

The changes not only improve the organization of the passage—indeed, they create an entirely different one—but they also clarify its relationship to the subsequent dominant

115. Regularity is further emphasized by the fact that essentially each measure presents one statement of the turn motive on one tone of the arpeggio.

Example 33

pedal preparation for the recapitulation. In Version 1 the most problematic aspect of the harmonic motion is the C_2^4 chord at measure *165ff*. By its contrast with the local stability of the first two four-measure units, the goal-directedness of the dominant seventh chord disturbs the uniformity and placidity established initially. It ultimately robs the immediate preparation for the recapitulation (perhaps even the moment of articulation of the recapitulation itself) of its force. This is so for several reasons. First, although the V_2^4 chord disrupts the procession of stable segments, the melodic construction parallels that of preceding segments. This puzzling discrepancy between melodic and harmonic function is partly responsible for the disturbance mentioned above. Second, once the C_2^4 is heard, the Gb triad (mm. *161–64*) is reinterpreted as a Neapolitan in F minor and, as a result, the whole progression ($II^{b6}–V_2^{4}–I^{b3}$) powerfully establishes F minor as a goal. Consequently, the arrival of F minor (m. *169*) undercuts the higher-level motion of V (m. *173ff.*) to I (m. *185*) from the immediate retransition into the recapitulation.

Arrival at the dominant pedal (m. *173*) in Version 1 is weak because it occurs as the end of a plagal progression, one that is seemingly circular and redundant: $V^7–I^{b3}–V^7–I$ (recapitulation). Moreover, when first heard, the strongest bass tone, the low C (m. *173*), may be understood as simply a continuation of the cello's descending arpeggio of F minor (F–C–Ab–F/C)—not particularly marked as a point of articulation. Thus the C_2^4 at measures *165–68* generates problems whose consequences are felt on the next higher level of articulation. If we are to judge from his revisions, Beethoven was indeed dissatisfied with the lack of articulation at the beginning of the dominant pedal passage in Version 1 (m. *173*).

The harmonic organization of measures 151–57 in Version 2 is markedly different in its own internal coherence as well as in its relationship to subsequent events. In the light of the discussion of Version 1, it should be clear that the elimination of the four-measure segment on the dominant of F minor and its replacement by F minor (m. 159, cf. m. *165*, Version 1)

Example 33 (continued)

constitute perhaps the single most important harmonic change. Approached by its Neapolitan, G♭, and given only *one* beat of dominant seventh harmony (first inversion, beat 3, m. 158), F minor is not only less stable and more processive than it is in Version 1, but its occurrence here also makes possible other important relationships both within the passage and between this passage and the next one: (1) B♭ minor–G♭ major//F minor–D♭ major; (2) the Neapolitan relationship G♭–f paralleled by D♭–C.[116] (Whereas G♭ moves to F minor, D♭ moves to C major, and this contrast makes the dominant [C] all the brighter and more forceful.) There is patterning, then, both within the segment and straddling this segment (the plateau) and the next (the retransition). F minor is in a pivotal position:

$$b♭ \; - \; G♭ \; - \; f \; - \; D♭ \; - \; C$$

Version 2: (b♭) I – VI – V$^{♭3}$ } or $\overline{b♭ - G♭} - \underline{f - D♭} - C(V^7)$

  (F) I$^{♭3}$ – ♭VI – V^7

Within the segment it is heard as a beginning; *after* the dominant pedal is reached (m. 167), it is heard as the end of one pattern—F minor as minor V in B♭ minor, similar to C major as V in F major. But in this *pivotal* position, F minor does not upstage the grand arrival of F major at the recapitulation.[117]

The nature of the harmonic patterning in the revised version is also underlined by changes in texture, rhythm, and melody. Texturally, one of the big differences between the two versions is the continuous buildup in the density of activity in Version 1 versus a kind of flat bipartite arrangement in Version 2.[118] In Version 1 there is a textural and rhythmic crescendo created by the gradual addition of voices and the increase in the degree of activity from one four-measure segment to the next: two voices, then three (including a new figure), then four (including a stretto-like figure similar to the one added in the second four

(See p. 67 for notes 116–118.)

measures), and finally a still more active four-part texture; the last results from the inversion of the original accompaniment pattern, appearing here in a prominent register of the first violin, as a pianistic volley between the tones of the descending minor sixth (Ab–C). (The original accompaniment figure, m. *157ff.*, was a simple pianistic seesaw of a minor third in the middle register of the second violin.) This composed crescendo is underlined in its final stage by a dynamic marking of "crescendo."

Contrasting with the mounting agitation of this sixteen-measure crescendo, the comparable passage in Version 2 is understated. It is characterized by a tightly controlled marshalling of four-measure units so that there is a clear articulation at the center, with no escalation of intensity. The accompanimental activity of Version 1 is relaxed—"flattened out," as it were—to the lulling reiteration of a single two-note chord that is much more violinistic.

The textural arrangements emphasize harmonic symmetry and also underline the processive position of the F minor segment, which has the same texture as the first segment in Bb minor. Moreover, in Version 2 Beethoven is careful to stress the beginnings of each four-measure group in the *same* fashion, with *forte-piano* marks. The instrumentation of each segment also holds action in check: the first violin has the main line for the first and third measure-groups, the second violin for the second and fourth. The addition of the cello's ♩ in the second and fourth segments enriches sonority while emphasizing symmetrical patterning between eight-measure units.

In Version 2 the rhythmic groupings complement the harmonic patterning (mm. 151–67). Because of the flattening out of the accompanimental figure, the first and third four-measure groups are mobile but not anacrustic to immediately following ones. Only the second and fourth—each with its Neapolitan- and dominant-function harmonies underlined by the added cello line—move as anacruses to the third unit and to the dominant pedal (m. 167), respectively.[119] In Version 1, on the other hand, there is a sameness of phrase-grouping: each fourth measure is written as an anacrusis to the beginning of the following group as ♫♫♫♫ | ♩ ♫♫ (see second violin, mm. *160–61*; viola, mm. *164–65*; and viola to cello, mm. *168–69*). The groupings are essentially alike, and the whole sixteen-measure passage lacks large-scale shape.

Foreground rhythm: a miscast upbeat figure is deleted.

On lower levels of rhythmic activity, the premature occurrence of the figure ♪♫♩ within the sixteen-measure plateau in Version 1 creates enormous problems. The figure is problematic both in its own immediate context and in relation to what follows in the dominant pedal passage. First, the immediate context: because the first four-measure segment is without it, the figure introduced in the second segment, and its increased presence in the third and fourth segments, not only disturbs the "calm" but actually escalates activity to a virtual "agitato." As Daniel Gregory Mason put it: "This restless figure . . . enters a dozen measures earlier [than in Version 2] like a blue-bottle fly spoiling the quiet of a lazy summer afternoon! Such miscasting of characters never appears in Beethoven after he had once 'learned how to write quartets properly.'"[120] Partly because of its prominent registral position, the ♪♫♩ figure articulates measure-to-measure action. The hyperactivity in these measures is increased by the action of the broken figure (in the accompaniment of the lowest part in the first three phrases and in the first violin line in the last phrase). This overarticulation within and between measures tends to detract from the pendular action of hypermeasures[121]—the swing of four-measure modules. As such, it distracts us from the regularity of harmonic change.

116. The motion D♭–C occurs in the same way (with just one beat of V$^6_5$ harmony just before C) that the motion G♭ to F occurred.

117. The harmonic revisions in this passage also emphasize that, at least in retrospect, the large-scale motion of the whole development is understood as a progression from IV (B♭) to V (C), implying the tonic (F) at the beginning of the recapitulation. This harmonic plan is, of course, a common one for developments in classic music.

118. The first two segments of four measures parallel the second two in instrumentation, number of participating voices, and the melodic patterning at the end of each "half" of the passage (i.e., mm. 158 and 166).

119. Note that in Version 2, in the middle of the sixteen-measure segment, the Neapolitan moves to V$^6_5$ and then to the temporary tonic, whereas at the end, the dominant-function harmony is in the much more unstable position of VII[7].

120. Mason, *Quartets of Beethoven*, p. 23.

121. I borrow the term "hypermeasure" from Edward T. Cone, *Musical Form and Musical Performance*, p. 79. "Hypermeasure" is Cone's felicitous description for "measures [that] combine into phrases that are themselves metrically conceived. . . . These almost demand to be counted as units." The measure behaves as a beat.

The presence of the upbeat figure in the plateau also causes longer-range problems. These include upstaging its later appearance in the dominant pedal passage (m. *173ff.*/167ff., Ex. 34).[122] In both versions of the pedal passage, Beethoven makes the measure the unit of motion and focuses attention on internal rhythmic tensions. In Version 2 the shift in the prevailing unit of action from the four-measure hypermeasure to the one-measure unit is an important agent for the drive toward the recapitulation. In Version 1, because the ♪♫♩ figure gives prominence to the measure qua unit in the plateau, the contrast in the motion from hypermeasure to measure between the plateau and the retransition is decidedly weaker. Also, because there is motivic repetition and continuity in Version 1 instead of contrast, the dominant pedal passage lacks new forward thrust. The escalation of tension has simply come too soon in Version 1. In his revision Beethoven corrected this problem in the "timing" of events.

One final point about the miscast upbeat figure: its registral prominence does not allow it to be easily subsumed into an accompanimental background. Indeed, register and instrumentation call attention to the gaucheries of part-writing; voices repeatedly get in one another's way. To take one striking example: the high B♭ (m. *164*, Version 1) moving to E (beat 1, m. *165*) strongly implies resolution to F—but too soon. The tensional quality here is too strong for this moment in the structure. When the F is finally heard (in the lower parts, m. *169*), its placement in the low register saves the process from too great a closure for this formal moment. But, then, retrospectively the motion from the high B♭ down to E seems an empty theatrical gesture, an intensity completely misplaced. Moreover, once in that high register in the second segment of the plateau, what is left for the third and fourth? Because of their texture, the third and fourth segments seem otherwise calculated to produce further escalation of activity. But the second segment has, as it were, preempted the dramatic register too early. What remains in the fourth segment is a kind of pointless agitation, particularly that of the A♭–C in the first violin. This is better understood in comparison with the careful staging of the high B♭ (and its motion to E) that Beethoven saves for the close of the dominant pedal preparation in Version 2 (mm. 175–76, in Ex. 34).

122. Mason writes: "A . . . striking example of the disastrous results of misplacing a right thing" (*Quartets of Beethoven*, p. 23).

Retransition

Preparatory function is set in high relief through revisions of rhythm and part-writing.

The final segment of the development, the retransition to the recapitulation, is a twelve-measure dominant pedal passage in both versions.[123] Since harmony is basically the same, other parameters are responsible for differences between the two versions—differences in the sense of contained tension, in directional drive, and in the anacrustic thrust of the whole passage.

Even before the passage is under way in Version 1, the beginning has been robbed of some of its anacrustic power. The earlier presence of the ♪𝅘𝅥𝅮𝅘𝅥𝅮𝅘𝅥 figure detracts from its effectiveness; that is, the kind and level of energy add nothing new, and, because the plagal approach is weak, there is little new momentum generated at the beginning of the pedal segment. The revisions suggest that Beethoven also considered the internal nature of the passage less than satisfactory in Version 1. The articulation of the entire passage into 4 + 8 measures (in both versions) makes this same division a convenient one for discussion.

123. In Version 2 the similarities between kinds of motion into the retransition (mm. 166–67) and into the last phase of the transition in the exposition (mm. 48–49; see Exx. 4 and 10) suggest a general correspondence in layout and, to some extent, proportions between the exposition and development. In short, as the following chart indicates, Beethoven's revisions result in quite close correspondences in overall lengths:

	8				21						20 = 49	
Mm.:			4	2	2	4	2	5	2			
Exp:	1–6	7–8	9–12	13–14	15–16	17–20	21–22	23–27	28–29	....		30–49
Dev:	119–25	126–28	....	129–34	135–40	....	141–46	....	147–48	149–50	151–67	
Mm.:				6	6		6		2	2		
	10				22						17 = 49	

The correspondences suggested in the chart may of course be mere coincidence. But that they may be more than mere fiction is, supported by motivic and other similarities between measures 1–8 and 119–28; harmonic similarities between measures 13–29 and 129–50, discussed on pp. 48–49; comparable harmonic progressions between measures 40–41–49 (C–A♭–G as V of C) in the exposition, and measures 151–55 and especially measures 159–163–167 (f–D♭–C as V of F) in the development; textural similarities between measures 30–48 and 151–66; and similarities in line and texture between measures 48–49 and 166–67. It is particularly striking that the total lengths from the beginning of the correspondences to the end are, in both cases, forty-nine measures. (If one accepts this as significant, it may also help to account for the "added" two measures in Version 2 [mm. 147–48], because without these the forty-nine measure correspondence would not be exact.)

Example 34

BEETHOVEN'S COMPOSITIONAL CHOICES

The presence of the ♪♫♩ figure in the *midst* of measures in Version 1 tends to emphasize beat 3 (see Ex. 34). When heard in conjunction with the very same pattern straddling the bar-line and with the offbeat patterning in the first violin, the figure (beat 2 to beat 3) confuses the basic metric grouping. The downbeat of the measure is not clear and forward momentum is diffused.[124]

In Version 2 (m. 167ff.) Beethoven finds a way to propel motion forward while keeping the downbeat of the measure—and the drive of its regular recurrence—clearly in focus. He removes the figure that occurs in the midst of the measures (mm. *173–76/167–70*) and reserves it for delineation of the meter. The sforzando on the third beat (C) of the first violin line[125] strengthens the motion across the bar-line and provides fresh momentum for each successive pattern beginning on the high C. Without the sforzando (mm. *173–74* of Version 1), the tone C on beat 3 fails to sustain momentum across the bar-line. The C is weak here because of its register, its position in the meter, and its place at the end of a rhythmic group. In Version 2, additionally, the sforzando on beat 2 (inner voices) animates these measures internally while the cello's sforzando promotes motion across the bar-line. But though each beat of the measure is stressed in Version 2, the downbeats are the weightiest and keep the notated meter primary.

Differences in the disposition of the parts and the resultant sonorities also heighten the sense of contained tension, of impending arrival, in the first part of the dominant pedal passage. Present in Version 2, but lacking in Version 1, is the rich, middle-register sound of C_4^6 (viola and second violin, mm. 167–71). The reiteration of this central core of sound, in the same rhythmic position, insists on the *non*-movement of harmony. The sonority emphasizes the enchainment in the unstable harmony and the urgent need for resolution.

Aside from its rhythmic consequences, the registral position of the accompanimental figure ♪♫♩ in Version 1 tends to cover the important line in the first violin and thus to diffuse directional drive.[126] The registral problem in Version 1 is especially acute in measures *175–76*. There the high C and E in the second violin, and the high E in the viola, obscure the sixteenth-note pattern in the first violin and make it difficult to notice the stretto effect created by the beginning of that same pattern again on beat 3. It is important that the stretto effect not be clouded here for two reasons: (1) it immediately intensifies the activity that had been charged but "running in place," a kind of braked tension; and (2) the pattern's beginning here serves as a signal of the imminent change at measure *177*. In contrast, the revised part-writing in Version 2 makes the direction and drive of the outer parts clearly audible.

The revisions of the last eight measures of the dominant pedal passage (mm. *177–84/ 171–78*) transform a rhythmically square and lumpish passage with little goal-direction and drive, into a tightly focused, grand anacrustic sweep. Here the revisions in rhythmic patterning, melodic line, register, voice-leading, and texture are especially closely inter-related.

The problems with Version 1 are most serious immediately preceding the recapitulation (mm. *181–84*). At the beginning of the passage (m. *177f.*), the rhythm in the violins has little

---

124. The patterns of the two inner parts, on the one hand, and that of the cello, on the other, equalize one another, particularly since the one in the inner parts is doubled. It would seem from his revisions that in both versions Beethoven wanted to give impetus to the third beat of the measure in the first violin part, but his solution in Version 1 merely accents the third beat without making it mobile.

125. The Mies edition in the new *Werke* places the first violin's sforzando in measures 167–69 on the *second* beat of each measure. Since there is no "Revisionsbericht" for the new *Werke* and since this placement makes so little sense, here I am following Breitkopf & Härtel's *Gesamtausgabe*, ser. 6, vol. 1, no. 37. In the latter edition, the sforzando appears on the third beat in the first violin part in measures 167–68 and does not appear in measure 169.

126. This was also the case in the previous segment, the plateau, at measure *161ff.*

DEVELOPMENT

forward momentum. The dotted half-note calls attention to the measure; indeed, the measure temporarily becomes the beat here. Although the passage is ongoing, the uniformity of the measure-to-measure motion in the upper parts generates no rhythmic instability; the lack of differentiation in rhythmic durations creates no groupings. Melodically, the ascending diminished triad (E–G–B♭, beginning on B♭) itself establishes no unmistakable, to say nothing of urgent, goals.[127]

The lower parts (mm. *177–80*) are superficially less uniform, less stodgy in their motion. Their seeming instability, however, results at least partly from the rhythmic-metric confusion that reigns rather than from any genuine tension. The melodic patterning previously heard in the first violin (mm. *173–76*) is now made the subject (mm. *177–80*) of an essentially regular dialogue between the cello and the viola, at the interval of *two* beats. The beginning of each two-beat unit in the lower parts is stressed by dynamics on beats 1 and 3 (m. *177*), 2 (m. *178*), 1 and 3 (m. *179*), and 2 (m. *180*). Thus, in the two lower parts there is a kind of displacement of the given meter—from triple to duple. This in turn effects a weak metric conflict between the two lower parts on the one hand and the two upper ones on the other. But there is still another element of conflict and confusion in patterning. Each module of the dialogue consists of a kind of hypermeasure of four beats (cello for two, then viola for two). The reiteration of this pattern creates yet another patterning: three hypermeasures of four beats each, stretched across four measures of three beats each. This, too, is a source of confusion in the given context. But even this hypermeasure grouping lacks real clarity because of slight inconsistencies in internal patterning.[128] These disturbances of uniformity impinge on the organization of hypermeasures.

One other agent of the confusion that suffuses this passage in Version 1 is the muddiness of sound created by the registral placement of the dialogue. The sound of the open C string in the viola (mm. *178–81*) and cello (mm. *179–81*) tends to cover some of the dialogue patterning because the whole dialogue is set low, especially at the sforzandi in the open strings.[129]

In one sense, then, events from measure *177* to the end of measure *180* have the quality of "running in place." At the end of measure *180* there is only minimal momentum (created by the lower parts) and no new impulses or signs of change. By the end of this measure, the upper voices have moved through one octave of the melodic diminished triad (from its fifth, B♭ to B♭) and the first violin continues through the same triad (again beginning on the fifth). But this continuation generates no new goals. The change in the accompaniment, including the reversal of direction of the sixteenth-note patterning (the imitative dialogue) in the lower parts at measure *181*, does, however, create a light articulation.[130]

127. Note that I refer here to the melodic line per se, not to the larger context of dominant harmony (of which the line is a part). More will be said about the continuation of the melodic line in the first violin.

128. A modest internal subdivision is created both by the motion to the low C in the cello, beat 1, measure *179*—after that tone had not been heard in the bass since measure *173*—and by the fact that the sixteenth-note pattern first begins on G but subsequently on C (m. *179ff.*). The same sort of inconsistency had occurred at measure *174*, as compared with measure *173*. Indeed, in measure *173* there is no clear initial indication that the pattern does not begin on the downbeat rather than on the second sixteenth-note; the patterning becomes clear only at measure *174*.

129. Here the regular dialogued alternation of the two-beat exchange between viola and cello seems related to register. Beethoven evidently wanted to maintain the basic melodic patterning established in the first violin in measures *173–76*. But dovetailing was not possible because in this register (viola and cello) it would have produced virtual chaos. In Version 2, both contrary motion and registral separation (second violin instead of viola) make dovetailing viable. And the overlapping is appropriate because the second violin supports the rhythm of the syncopated upper parts even while it complements the motivic structure of the cello.

130. There is less muddiness in register here and this dialogue is heard more clearly than that at measures *177–80*.

Final motion into the recapitulation is intensified: melody, rhythm, and dynamics are revised.

The last four measures of the development in Version 1 doubtless rank among the most miscalculated in the entire movement (Ex. 34). The first violin continues up through the diminished triad, but instead of moving to the high B♭, which might have been a goal, it only reaches the high G (m. *182*); the subsequent skip from high G to low C is startling and seems abortive. Moreover, as discussed earlier, Beethoven had used up the high B♭—the highest pitch in the movement—prematurely, in a relatively unmarked place in the midst of the plateau (m. *164*).[131]

At the potential peak of tension, just before the return of F major, the cumulative unaltered pace and the absence of clearly defined goals spawn a schizoid diffusion of direction in line and a sudden loss of power in the forward impulse—just when it should be greatest. Given the handling of measures *177–82* in Version 1, there are now serious registral problems intricately connected with linear ones, as well as with the resulting degree of rhythmic thrust. Not only is it difficult to keep track of the lines, but the crossing of registers and lines in the two violin parts effect a reduction of the two parts to one in a hocket-like manner. Because they are covered by the high register tones, the low C in the first violin and the E in the second violin (beat 2, m. *183*) are not heard linearly: the "line" seems to move from the high G (first violin, m. *182*), to the G an octave below (second violin, beat 1, m. *183*), to the B♭ in the viola (beat 2, m. *183*).[132] The sforzando B♭ (second violin, m. *183* tied to m. *184*) is left hanging. Since the low E (beat 3, m. *184*) is barely audible, the "line" seems simply to drop to F (first violin, recapitulation) after a beat of silence. In short, linear direction is in doubt at the very moment that the target should be unequivocally clear.

In Version 2 Beethoven radically transforms the last eight measures of the development (mm. 171–78) so that their preparatory function is set in high relief.[133] From the very beginning of this segment, all elements seem sharply and clearly directed toward two goals, the first at measure 175, the second at measure 179 (the recapitulation). Before discussing the particular nature of the goal-direction, however, a few remarks on the overall internal context are pertinent.

In contrast to the *fortissimo* dynamic of the entire analogous passage in Version 1, the dynamic level of the passage in Version 2 is *piano*, with sforzando intensifications and a crescendo at the end. The *piano* here provides its own type of energy: that of hushed containment. In this context, the *piano* is one of a set of signs indicating the imminence of the *forte* return of the tonic. Texturally, the relationship among the four parts produces a more interlocked, meshed effect than does the polar arrangement of two upper versus two lower parts in Version 1. In Version 2 the pairing of first violin with viola locks the top and middle together, while the registral separation and concomitant contrary motion between the cello and second violin allows for a dovetailing of their patterns; this dovetailing, too, creates a more tightly knit texture (cf. the blocked dialogue of two-beat sixteenth-note patterns in the lower parts of Version 1). Finally, the continuous presence of the C major sound in the viola is a center of sound, a kind of hub, from which the contrary motion moves out.

131. Because the high B♭ was followed by E, he had also "used up" the tritone for F in its most brilliant registral position. Thus, even if he had continued on to the highest B♭ here, it would have been somewhat anticlimactic.

132. Middle C in the first violin (m. *183*) is covered by the G in the second violin; the E on beat 2 in the second violin is covered by the B♭ in the viola.

133. Referring generally to dynamic differences and to the syncopations and contrary motion, both Waack ("Beethovens F-dur Streichquartett Op. 18 No. 1," p. 419) and Wedig ("Beethovens Streichquartett op. 18 nr. 1," p. 21) comment on the heightened preparation for the recapitulation that Beethoven accomplishes in his revision. Kerman finds that even in Version 2 the preparation for the recapitulation is "frenetic" and "rather silly" (*Beethoven Quartets*, p. 35).

In the first four measures of the passage (mm. 171–74), the interactions of pitch, meter, rhythm, and dynamics combine to catapult action toward measure 175. Melodically, the outer parts, particularly that of the first violin, are most prominent. After the first beat (Bb), the ascending diminished triad is metrically displaced by syncopations cum dynamic stresses. The first octave (Bb) is reached in the midst of this displacement. When the melodic line continues its ascent through the same triad, the high Bb (m. 175) is the unmistakable goal. The motion toward it is intensified by the quarter-note action (the high E and G, m. 174) that breaks out of the syncopated patterning. This articulates a local anacrusis (to m. 175) within the higher-level one, which has been ongoing from beat 2 of measure 171.[134] Thus, the Bb (m. 175), which is the melodic peak of the movement, is not only the realization of immediate melodic goals but, occurring as it does on the downbeat, is also the realization of a local rhythmic goal. It marks the first coincidence of a structural tone and a metric downbeat since beat 1, measure 171.

As the sharply highlighted realization of the melodic and rhythmic goals around which the first four measures of the passage had been organized, measure 175 is at once the height and the turning point of the process of return. The preceding stretto effect (in the second violin and cello; compare mm. 173–74 with mm. 171–72) and the hemiola in the cello (three two-beat scale patterns within two measures) intensify this articulation. The resumption of the sforzando in the three upper parts at measure 175 after its absence in measure 174 also underlines the articulation; the coincidence of the sforzando with the change in the direction of the cello line further underscores this moment.[135] In addition to the basic harmonic instability of measure 175, the registral disposition of the dominant seventh chord is particularly harsh: the seventh between the violins, the absence of a third in the chord, the perfect fourth between viola and second violin, the two octaves between cello and viola. In this context, the textural gap between the top and bottom is especially tensional and implicative of subsequent contrary motion toward the middle register.

In the last four measures of the development, the previous metric displacement (in first violin and viola, mm. 171–74) is replaced by regularity: the meter *is* the measure. Although the cello and second violin continue to have accent patterns noncongruent with the notated meter, the sound of the first violin dominates: its harmonic/melodic tension is the focus. The dip from the high Bb (m. 175) to E (m. 176) aims a "high beam" on the tritone for F. The absence of the E in the preceding chord has made its presence here (m. 176) especially forceful. The delay of F for two measures is particularly effective. The cumulative tension created by all aspects of patterning, including the added crescendo (mm. 177–78), and highlighted by the motion from E to G makes measure 178 a real "cliff-hanger."[136] Beethoven has carefully staged the moment of greatest tension (mm. 175–78) and the compelling convergence of all activity in the resolution that takes place at the beginning of the recapitulation.

134. Because of patterning and dynamic stresses that work against the measure, there is a minimal amount of sounded downbeat in measures 171–74 (as compared with a heavy emphasis on sounded downbeats in the corresponding passage in Version 1).

135. In the equivalent spot in Version 1 (mm. *180–81*), the reversal is less marked because the cello is tied.

136. As with the articulation that was signaled at measure 175, the absence of a sforzando after the first beat of measure 177, combined with the crescendo marking of measure 178, tends to heighten the effect of two measures united as one large upbeat to the recapitulation. The slur in the first violin also helps the grand sweep into the recapitulation. It is interesting to note that in Version 1 Beethoven used the slur for the measure (m. *176*) *before* the last eight, but not immediately before the recapitulation—exactly the reverse of Version 2. This bowing (Version 2) emphasizes consistency in the segment between measures 167 and 170. In Version 1 the inconsistency created by the change of bowing (the slur, first violin) at measure *176* detracts from the internal patterning of the first phrase of the retransition.

4

RECAPITULATION

RECALL OF KEY AREA I
(Measures *185–202/179–98*)

Both versions diverge from the exposition; revisions focus the harmonic process and clarify phrase structure.

Measures 185–202 179–98

In each version the first eight measures of the recapitulation are the same as those of the exposition. In both versions, too, a divergence from the order of events in the exposition follows.[137] This divergence or excursion (mm. *193–202/187–98*) represents, in both cases, a new direction as compared with events in the exposition and a kind of surrogate for the action that had taken place in measures 13–29. But although comparable, the excursions differ from one another significantly.[138] Each has its own effect upon the resumption of subsequent correspondences (between the exposition and recapitulation in each version) with the transition to the second key area.

Both excursions *end* in G♭ major (m. *202/198*); see Example 35. But the harmonic routes and the timing—in several senses of that word—are quite different. In Version 1 the initial motion to B♭, the subdominant (m. *193ff.*), establishes no clear harmonic goal; there is only the probability that it will be followed by dominant harmony.[139] The change of mode to B♭ minor (m. *197*) is primarily coloristic; and, while it is likely that its relative major will be heard, D♭ major is not set up as a goal. B♭ minor does, however, provide entrée to D♭, which is first heard pivotally in measure *200* (as III in B♭ minor and V in G♭ major) and then—but

137. Such developmental digressions are, of course, not uncommon in recapitulations in sonata form. One possible reason for the divergence here is suggested by Basil Lamm in *Beethoven String Quartets 1*, BBC Music Guides (Seattle, 1975), p. 14: "The attentive listener must wonder what is to become of the expressive harmonies in bars 13–29 of the exposition. . . . Beethoven's already mature mastery guides him to leave out the whole section, which would be weakened in its effect by the powerful harmony of the development." Compare my text, pp. 48–49.

138. The brief sketch to the revision of this passage (staves 3 and 4, Landsberg 7) provides additional documentation for Beethoven's concern with the passage. (Recall that this is one of only two sketched passages that are unequivocally for the revised version.) Kramer, "The Sketches for Opus 30," p. 143, writes that this sketch clinches the move to B♭ minor.

139. And when the subdominant sequence of material in measures *189–92* is heard, there is no real indication of how far the sequence may be taken; nor is the impending excursion implied.

Example 35

for only one measure—as a clear dominant for G♭ (m. *201*). The arrival at G♭ is weak, in short, because of the harmonic approach; it is also weak because of action in other parameters, which will be discussed below.[140]

In Version 2 the excursion (mm. 187–98) telescopes the route through B♭ minor and moves to successive half-cadences in D♭ major (mm. 190, 192). In prospect, D♭ becomes the predominant tonal center of the passage. Its prominence makes motion to G♭ more probable than it is in Version 1, despite the fact that D♭ becomes a clear dominant for G♭ (as V^7) only at measure 197 (being, in this respect, analogous to Version 1). By reiterating the cadence of the first phrase, the two added measures (mm. 191–92, inserted between mm. *196–97* of Version 1) underline the motion to D♭ (IV–V), but with a stronger half-cadence this second time. Thus, in Version 2, D♭ major is given some relative autonomy. Although internally the same as the corresponding measures in Version 1 (mm. *197–98*), because of their changed context, the two measures in B♭ minor in Version 2 (mm. 193–94) are heard as a coloristic excursion from D♭ rather than B♭ major. Retrospectively, the entire passage in Version 2 is understood in relation to G♭.[141]

The measure-groupings that result from the revisions of this passage (mm. *193–202/* 183–98) also clarify the nature of the motion toward G♭ and emphasize its arrival. These groupings in analogous passages may be diagrammed as follows:

Version 1:   mm. *193   194   195   196   197   198   199   200   201   202*

```
                    ┌──────────────────────────────────────────────────┐
                         ┌─────────┐
                              2
                    └─────────────────┘ └───────────┘ └──────────────────┘
                              4         +     2      +          4
```

Version 2:   mm. 187   188   189   190   191   192   193   194   195   196   197   198

```
                 1  +  1  +     2      +     2      +     2      +        4
              └──────────────────────┘ └──────────┘└────────────────────────────┘
                     ┌ ─ ─ ─ ─ ─ ─ ─ ─ ─ ─ ─ ─ ─ ─ ┤└ ─ ─ ─ ─ ─ ─ ─ ─ ─ ─ ─ ─ ─ ┘
```

primary grouping   ─────
secondary grouping   --------

As is partly evident from the diagram, the grouping in Version 1 does not cumulate or move toward the articulation at measure *202*; quite the contrary, rhythmic tension tends to dissipate in the center (mm. *197–98*), and there is no subsequent restoration of momentum. Because they are understood as a "complete unit" that is sequentially related to the preceding phrase, the first four measures (mm. *193–96*) in Version 1 are heard as a single relatively stable block rather than as 2 + 2 measures.[142] Further, both measures *197–98* and *199–200* tend to be heard as echoes of measures *195–96*, with the second echo extended and integrated with measures *200–201* to lead to the cadence in G♭.

In Version 2 the immediate articulation of the phrase (beginning at m. 187) created by the one-measure sequence (mm. 187 to 188) means that, instead of being heard simply as a four-measure grouping (2 + 2), measures 187–90 are heard as a more cumulative 1 + 1 + 2. This is important for several reasons. First, the change from the preceding patterning is a clear sign that the movement will not continue as it has; that is, we are cued almost from the beginning. Second, the grouping of 1 + 1 + 2 (mm. 187–90) is then doubled to 2 + 2 + 4 (mm. 191–98). The rhythmic cumulation in the four-measure unit is implied once the pattern of 2 + 2 (mm. 191–94) is heard. In addition to the measure-grouping that makes G♭ (m. 198) a strong goal in Version 2, the anacrustic rhythm of the first

(See p. 78 for notes 140–142.)

violin in measure 196, and of the cello in measure 197, intensifies closure in G♭ at measure 198; compare this with the much weaker rhythmic motion in the analogous parts of Version 1. The crescendo of measures 196–97 further heightens the motion toward measure 198, while the deceptive dynamic of *piano*, at precisely the time when the goal is realized (m. 198), marks the moment especially.[143] By comparison, the swell in the three lower parts of Version 1 (mm. *200–201*) is a rather empty *empfindsamer* gesture—an expressive inflection without any real relation to the syntax of the moment.[144]

Again echoes clarify local form.

Aside from their role in providing a changed measure- and phrase-grouping, the two added measures (mm. 191–92) in Version 2 clarify what is statement and what is echo by creating a kind of statement-counterstatement relationship between measures 191–192 (in their relationship to mm. 189–90) and measures 195–96 (in their relationship to mm. 193–94). Thus, what seemed to be a "parentless" echo in Version 1 (mm. *199–200*)—weak in function, as an echo to an echo—is given a raison d'être in Version 2. Indeed, the relationship of measures 191–92 and measures 195–96 to their preceding pairs, as well as to each other, underlines the syntax of these measures.

An understanding of the two added measures as echoes also makes clear the parenthetical nature of measures 191–92 and 195–96 to the basic linear motion (treble) in Version 2 (Ex. 36). In short, syntax is underlined by character and vice-versa. The echoes,

Example 36

registrally separated from the rest of the passage, are clarified qua echoes when one understands that they are not part of the main line. In Version 1 the role of measures *197–98* is confused (Ex. 35). On the one hand, because of their modified echo of measures *195–96* these measures are heard as parenthetical; on the other, because of register, they are heard as part of the main linear motion. The principal melodic line of Version 1 is confused in other ways as well, for the figuration of the first violin part in measure *195* diffuses and buries the implicit linear descent that is clear in Version 2.

Textural revisions are coordinated with all the changes discussed above to enhance the

140. Kramer, "The Sketches for Opus 30," p. 142, concurs that "the preparation for G♭ seems peculiarly unstable." He finds the revision of this passage similar to that of measures 129–33 in the finale (p. 143). Beethoven may have had in mind recreating the effect of a cadence to ♭VI in B♭ (i.e., G♭) in a way that would be reminiscent of the motion to A♭ in the context of C major at measure 41 in the exposition.

141. In one sense, because the passage begins by indicating B♭ minor and returns to this key in its course (mm. 193–94), there is an effect of a gentle volley between the major (D♭) and its relative minor, although the major is the primary point of harmonic reference. Wedig refers to this passage in Version 2 as a kind of self-enclosed ring that has an organic effect because the first part in D♭ major points to the coming G♭, while the second passage, in B♭ minor, looks back to D♭ (Wedig, "Beethovens Streichquartett op. 18, nr. 1," p. 21).

142. However, the new figuration in the first violin modifies the nature of the passage in a somewhat baffling way, both because the figuration is new here and because it is never heard again in the movement. Also, because of its register, the figuration partly covers the main melodic line in the second violin and in so doing tends to obscure the integrity of the four-measure unit. Other consequences of this figuration are discussed below.

syntax of the passage. The initial revisions of texture are part of the aggregation of signs indicating that what follows measure 185 is indeed an excursion and not primarily a block-variant of previous events. In Version 1 measures *193–96* are texturally similar to measures *189–92*.[145] In Version 2, however, the absence of the cello in measures 187–90 and the disposition of the parts coordinate with the measure-grouping to clearly signify the break with the immediately preceding events. The textural contrast provided by the added two-measure echo in Version 2 (mm. 191–92) helps to establish structural parallelism between measures 191–92 and 195–96, on the one hand, and measures 189–90 and 193–94, on the other.

RECALL OF TRANSITIONAL MATERIAL
(Measures *202–26*/198–216)

Telescoping fuses two aspects of the transition: new long-range connections between the exposition and recapitulation.

Measures 202–20 198–210

In both versions the G♭ major passage (Ex. 37, mm. *202ff.*/198ff.) is structurally analogous to the passage beginning on A♭ major (as ♭VI in C, m. 41) in the exposition. But to varying degrees in each version, the G♭ major passage also fulfills part of the function of the passage from measures 30 to 41 (first violin motive). In Version 2 we recognize, almost from the beginning of the passage, that measure 198ff. is simultaneously related to measure 30ff. *and* to measure 41ff. In Version 1, however, while the relationship of measure *202* to measure *41* is clear initially, the reference to action from measures *30* to *41* is revealed only subsequently. Thus, measure *202ff.* corresponds to measure *41ff.*, measures *208–9* are reminiscent of measures *35–36*, and measure *211ff.* is comparable to measure *30ff.* The greater length of the whole passage in Version 1 (six measures longer than that in Version 2) is, of course, partly a function of this successive—if sequentially reversed—recall of events of the exposition.

The principal revision of the passage consists in a telescoping or compression of action that, in the exposition, had occurred in two stages: measures 30–41; and measures 41–49. While the preeminent aspect of measure 198ff. in Version 2 is a correspondence with measure 41ff., primarily because of the action in the three lower parts, the first violin part is most like that at measure 31ff.; so, too, is the "wait" for the melody to join the accompaniment (cf. mm. 29–30 with mm. 198–99). The result is a fusion of two aspects of the transition.[146] This fusion is possible in Version 2 largely because in his revision of the exposition Beethoven had made more palpable connections between the material in measures 30–41 and that in measures 41–47, notably the inclusion of the appoggiatura in the melodic lines of *both* segments (see above, p. 14). This had not been the case in Version 1 where the transition was problematic partly because of the melodic differences between successive passages—i.e., the very lack of conformance between measures *30–41* and *41–47*.

143. The *p* here has the effect of a deceptive cadence (harmonically); as such, it calls attention to this moment (see above for the earlier example of this role of a *pp*).

144. In Version 1 only the first violin has the crescendo to a *piano*, as found in Version 2; not supported by the same dynamics in other voices, this effect is simply not strong enough to be heard.

145. Except in the viola. There the eighth-note division of the root of the chord does suggest a difference from the preceding passage; but this difference is not made clear by other parameters.

146. The trill figure makes the correspondence with measure 30 the clearest, but the appoggiatura figure in measures 200, 202, 204 relates both to measures 31, 33, 35 and to measures 43, 45.

RECAPITULATION

Example 37

BEETHOVEN'S COMPOSITIONAL CHOICES

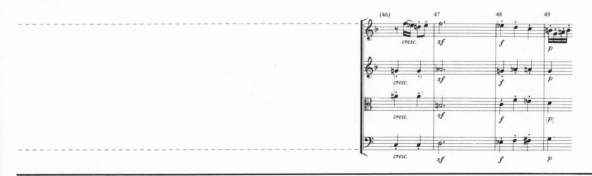

One of the interesting aspects of the correspondences between the exposition and recapitulation in Version 1 is that one can almost "see" Beethoven's gradual recognition of the possible relationships between material in measures *30–41* and that in measures *41–47*, a recognition that would seem to have led to revisions of the exposition in Version 2. In the recapitulation of Version 1, unlike its exposition, the material originally heard at measure *30ff.* (including the appoggiatura figure) is heard as a varied restatement of the material from measure *41ff.* (missing the appoggiatura in the exposition). The order is reversed here (m. *202ff.* is like m. *41ff.*, m. *211ff.* like m. *30ff.*); yet the similarity of the two passages is made more explicit than it was in the exposition (Version 1).[147] Somewhat paradoxically, perhaps, the compressed version, Version 2, seems more like the transition in the exposition than does the fuller Version 1.

In Version 1 the varied restatement of the passage in G♭ (cf. m. *202ff.* with m. *210ff.*) results in a very long stretch of one basic texture (fourteen measures, mm. *202–15*). Such textural placidity and stability last far too long in a passage that is, after all, analogous to the transition in the exposition. For unlike the exposition, in which the raison d'être for the first part of the transition (mm. *30–41*) is the harmonic motion from F to A♭ (as ♭VI in C), the decisive harmonic motion here—to G♭ (as Neapolitan in F), a deflection analogous to ♭VI in the exposition—has already occurred by the very beginning of the passage (m. *202*). The continuation of the passage in varied restatement accomplishes nothing except the filling out of the structural length that had occurred in the corresponding passage of the exposition. Indeed, Beethoven may have "backtracked" to the material from measure *31* in Version 1 precisely because he was concerned with the proportions of structure as set in the exposition.

One of the consequences of the sheer length of the G♭ major passage in Version 1 is that the key and texture, as well as the overall character of the passage, become stabilized; such stability is misplaced in this context.[148] To move out of this lull—fourteen measures of relatively slow paced action, harmonic changes every two measures, and the continuous ornamental dominant pedal—requires a rather extreme and sudden acceleration of the pace of activity. Beethoven creates such acceleration both with an abrupt shift to beat-to-beat action (mm. *216–18*), which is generated by the patterning of second violin and viola, and with the bass line and harmony that now change every measure instead of every two measures. Three measures of this increased activity lead to the resumption of stricter correspondences between the exposition and the recapitulation (measures *48ff.* and *219ff.*).

But for all the mock-furious activity, there is comparatively little anacrustic drive to the cadence on C (m. *220*). Rhythmic groups are contained within the measure from measures *216* through *218*. The sforzandi in Version 1 emphasize each measure qua unit rather than its grouping with other measures. In comparison to Version 2, there is a lack of strong forward motion; as a result, measure *218* does not move across the bar-line to the full measure of anacrusis in measure *219*. Indeed, the overall grouping is not very cumulative or goal-directed.

147. Beethoven may have realized the desirability for similarity as he worked this out in Version 1. (But he never went back to change the exposition.) He went this one step further in the exposition in Version 2 (see pp. 13–15) and this in turn provided an opportunity to go yet another step in the recapitulation of Version 2. Thus, successive sections of the completed versions show increasingly greater conformance of the two passages; in the excursions the function of the two passages is ultimately fused.

148. In Version 1 the passage seems like an episode in itself, whereas in Version 2 it assumes the quality of a transition from G♭ to C as dominant.

Consequences of telescoping include syntactic allusion, clearer signs, and the establishment of registral continuity.

In Version 2 the move from the passage in G♭ to the "perch" on C (as dominant for the rhyme with the second key area)[149] is accomplished with a far less drastic contrast (especially texturally and rhythmically) than in Version 1, and in an altogether tighter and more integrated fashion. There is a strong anacrusis to the cadence on C at measure 210 (bracketed in Ex. 37). The sequential linear descent from measure 206 is far more goal-directed than the bass line in Version 1 (mm. *216–18*), with its diminished fourth.

The sense of closure at measure 210 in Version 2 is also enhanced by what might be called "syntactic allusion." Because the first violin line of measures 207–8 resembles that of measures 183–84 (Ex. 35),[150] in rhythmic shape as well as the presence of a descending major sixth, and because in the earlier case a half-close followed in two measures, by association a half close in two measures is implied—and realized—here.[151] Thus, in several notable respects the revisions in the last four measures of the passage (ending with m. *220/210*) intensify the process as well as the coherence of this segment of the movement.

One further point about the approach to C (as dominant) in both versions. It concerns the nature of the cues Beethoven gives. In Version 2 (m. 207, in the first violin), the leap upward from the B♭, the main note of the turn pattern, to the G (m. 208) is a sign of the imminent change in action—that is, the imminent break with the excursion (and the presumed resumption of the rhyme with the exposition). At the same time, the interval (ascending major sixth) is a familiar one in this movement and is thus not in itself a radical break. While the stepped-up rhythmic activity in the analogous moment in Version 1 (from m. *216ff.*) is also a sign of the forthcoming change, these final measures (mm. *216–20*) do not seem related to any single passage in the exposition.[152] Their novelty is somewhat confusing in this context. Is something new about to occur? In short, although Beethoven cues us to impending change in both versions, the overanimated cues in Version 1 are somehow disproportionate to what follows.

Comparing the six-measure passages of dominant preparation for the rhyme with the second key area (Ex. 38), we may retrospectively infer yet another reason for the nature of the revision at the end of the preceding passage (Ex. 37, mm. *218–19/208–9*). The descending major sixth in the first violin of Version 2 (m. 208) may now be understood in this context not only for its syntactic allusion, but also because it serves to bring the first violin line into the "right" register for continuation—a continuation in which the many gaucheries of voice disposition and the concomitant rhythmic redundancies of Version 1 may now be eliminated. Similarly, the octave articulation of E in the cello on beat 3 of measure 208 in Version 2 is, in addition to its anacrustic function, a way of bringing the cello line up to a favorable position for the action in measures 210 and 212. The problematic aspects of the passage of dominant preparation in Version 1 (Ex. 38, mm. *220–26*) are especially plain to see. These stem, at least partly, from the registral position of the end of the preceding passage (mm. *218–19*).

149. Musical "rhyme" refers here to the similar sound but different harmonic (tonal) sense when melodic material from the second key area of the exposition is recalled in the recapitulation. I take this notion from Leonard G. Ratner. See his *Classic Music: Expression, Form, and Style* (New York, 1980), pp. 212 and 229.

150. Also, of course, measures 5–6.

151. It seems that such syntactic allusion is liable to be noticed in this context because the interval of the descending major sixth, as it occurs in the main melodic line, is exceptional in this movement. Indeed, the interval in this rhythmic shape was detached and isolated as an echo near the beginning of the development. And because measure 184 might have been continued at measure 209, it is possible, retrospectively, to view the entire excursion as parenthetical.

152. Or any other, elsewhere in the movement, for that matter.

Changes **within** ***Version 1 contribute to stasis.***

Taken as a group, the changes made from exposition to recapitulation *within* Version 1 exacerbate the already problematic aspects of the passage of dominant preparation for the second key area (and its tonic rhyme in the recapitulation). The voice-leading affects rhythm, pitch relationships (especially in the outer voices), and textures, all of which contribute to the near cessation of forward motion at the beginning of each measure.

The reiteration of the figure ♫|♩ in the cello (mm. *220–24*) is chiefly responsible for the halting effect. The heavy-handed emphasis on the downbeat (C) of each measure occurs even more often than in the corresponding passage of the exposition (Ex. 10, mm. *49–53*).[153] The pitch C (as the root of the chord) is ubiquitous, particularly in the motion across the bar-line. By comparison, the third rather than the root of the dominant chord helps to keep beat 1 mobile in both the exposition of Version 1 and the exposition and recapitulation of Version 2 (Exx. 10 and 38). Dynamics and texture also contribute to this halting effect in Version 1: *forte* and *fortissimo* and the regular textural massings on beats 1 and 3 of every measure emphasize arrival on the strong beats. As compared with the exposition, where dialogue is between first violin and cello, here the registral contrast in the measure-to-measure dialogue between violins is less, and so tends to diminish energy. That is, in comparison with both the exposition of the same version and the recapitulation of Version 2, the relationship among the concerting parts in the recapitulation of Version 1 contributes to stasis.

Beginning the anacrusis on the second half of beat 2 in the first violin may have been to compensate for the reiteration of the too prominent and insistent high C (heard across the bar-line, mm. *221–22, 223–24*).[154] But the enhanced anacrusis (as compared with the exposition in Version 1) is not much of a cure. Despite the anacrusis to the third beat and the greater motion it generates, the passage not only bogs down, but the reiteration of the high C also detracts from its later role in measure *226ff.* Interestingly, however, the necessity for the more mobile rhythmic figure here may have suggested the nature of the revisions in both exposition and recapitulation in Version 2.[155]

RHYME WITH KEY AREA II
(Measures *226–91/216–73*)

Modifications from exposition to recapitulation **within** ***Version 1 are carried over to both the exposition and recapitulation of Version 2.***

The passages that rhyme with the second key area (m. *226ff./216ff.*) are more alike in the recapitulations of both versions than they were in the expositions (m. 55ff.). This is because

Example 38

several notable modifications from exposition to recapitulation *within* Version 1 are carried over into both the exposition and recapitulation of Version 2. Since the exposition and recapitulation in Version 2 are virtually the same, except for the normal transposition in the recapitulation, I shall summarize the changes made *within* Version 1. The differences that remain between the two passages in the recapitulation (as compared with the two passages in the exposition) have already been considered in the discussion of the corresponding segments of the exposition (see pp. 18–25).

153. In the exposition, at least, the eighth-notes on the third beat of the measure moved to sixteenth-note motion (in dialogue with the first violin) and thereby provided melodic motion through the measure.

154. Here, in general, the reorchestration exacerbates the heaviness of the recurrent motion to the fifth (C).

155. Cf. measures *49–53* of Version 1 with measures *220–23* in the same version and with measures 49–53 of Version 2.

The main changes *within* Version 1 are as follows (see Exx. 12 and 39):

PHRASE 1 Second half of phrase (m. *229ff*., cf. m. *58ff*.): removal of cello part and the dominant pedal in the viola. Viola given cello line. This change is carried over to the exposition (and recapitulation) of Version 2.

PHRASE 2 Second half of phrase (mm. *233–35*, cf. mm. *62–65*): part-writing in upper parts changed and smoothed out to quarter-note motion, which conforms more with measures 242–43 than did corresponding passages in exposition. This change is carried over to the exposition of Version 2.

PHRASE 3 Not substantially changed. The high C, prominent as high pedal tone in the first violin, is heard for three beats instead of five and removed from the end of phrase 2 in the second violin.

PHRASE 4 Exchange of second violin and viola parts (m. *71*, cf. m. *242*). Removal of second beat from the very end of phrase in the first violin (m. *72*, beats 1 and 2; cf. m. *243*). This change is carried over to the exposition of Version 2.

The changes from exposition to recapitulation *within* Version 1 allow for more cumulative growth.[156] Both the lighter texture of the beginning and the more matched ends of phrases 2 and 4 create a somewhat higher-level relationship among phrases in the rhyme with the second key area. However, in his rewriting, Beethoven made the end of phrase 2 (Ex. 39, mm. *234–35*) *less* mobile than the analogous moment in the exposition (cf. Ex. 12, mm. *63–64*). (Perhaps it was because of this lack of mobility that in the exposition of Version 2 Beethoven reverted to the ending he had written for the comparable phrase in the exposition of Version 1.) The revision of the end of phrase 2 has a further consequence: namely, the sequential relationships of phrase endings that were potential in the exposition of Version 1—and realized as shaping forces in the exposition of Version 2 (see above, pp. 19–22, and Ex. 11)—are even more askew in the recapitulation than in the parallel passage in the exposition.

The remainder of the recapitulation essentially corresponds to the exposition of both versions.

---

156. With respect to discrepancies of this sort between the exposition and recapitulation, the first version of Op. 18, No. 1, first movement, is hardly a unicum. For example, Lockwood, "Beethoven: Opus 69," p. 43, writes of the autograph for Opus 69 (a *Fassung letzter Hand*): "When we find disagreements between apparently parallel passages in exposition and recapitulation it is sometimes difficult to decide if these are intentional and calculated subtleties, or if they are due to lapses in inserting corrections intended for both sections but actually inserted only in one."

Example 39

5

CODA

Measures
292–end
274–end

Revisions define character and clarify function; the turn motive is made a closing gesture.

Revisions of the coda clarify its function as a grand close for the movement and enhance the character of this final reinterpretation of the main melodic material of the movement, the initial turn motive (see Exx. 40 and 41). In Version 1 problematic choices for the disposition of the four parts, as well as the activity of the inner voices, have consequences for both the character and the structure of the coda.

The coda in both versions begins as a paraphrase of the early part of the development and becomes as *galant* as the development's fugato was learned (m. *300ff.*/m. 282ff.). Even without comparing the versions, the very beginning of the coda may be understood as a transposed recomposition of the final measures of the exposition. Our knowledge of the first and second endings of the recapitulation in Version 1 confirms this (Ex. 40).[157] In both versions, the first eight measures of the coda (mm. *292–99*/274–81) suggest a relationship with the development. In particular, they prepare us for the coda's paraphrase of the fugato (m. *300ff.*/282ff.). The ascending staccato scale in quarter-notes seems to be a reference to the ''countersubject'' of the fugato (see Ex. 28, m. *138ff.*/130ff., cello). Once this is recognized, the descending turn figures (shortened to ♫ , viola, Version 1; and first violin, Version 2) form a counterline that can be heard as a kind of *galant* jamming together of what had been the subject (♩ ♫♫) of the fugato.

The large-scale phrase organization is essentially the same in both versions; but *within* this, the phrase structure is clearer in Version 2. Although the important differences are within phrases and measure-groups, these also affect the clarity of the larger organization and heighten the cumulative effect of the coda in Version 2. The groupings may be diagrammed as follows (refer to Exx. 40 and 41):

157. The second ending in Version 1 (not present in Version 2, where there is no repeat of part II of the form) replaces the reiterated F major chord of the first ending. The move from F to D may be heard as analogous to the move from C to A, from the end of the exposition to the beginning of the development.

Version 1: mm. $\underline{\textit{300–303}}$ $\underline{\textit{304–11}}$ $\underline{\textit{312–17}}$ $\underline{\textit{318–20}}$

$$\underbrace{2 + 1 + 1}_{4} \; + \; \underbrace{2 + \overbrace{2 + 2}^{6} + 2}_{4} \; + \; \underbrace{(1+1) \; + \; (1+1) \; + \; 2}_{6} \; + \; 3$$

Version 2: mm. $\underline{282\text{–}85}$ $\underline{286\text{–}93}$ $\underline{294\text{–}99}$ $\underline{300\text{–}302}$

$$\underbrace{2 + 2}_{4} \; + \; \underbrace{2 + \overbrace{2 + 2}^{6} + 2}_{4} \; + \; \underbrace{2 + 2 + 2}_{6} \; + \; 3$$

Significant differences in grouping can be observed in the very first revised measures (Ex. 40, mm. *300–303/282–85*). In Version 1, despite the textural massing in measures *302–3*, the repetition of the turn motive, which is prominent because of register, emphasizes the separation of measures. In Version 2, on the other hand, the first statement of the turn motive is heard in relation to the descending triad that follows in the first violin; as a result, measures 284–85 are understood as statement and contrasting response. Although present in the viola (m. 285), the repetition of the turn motive is heard not as part of the main line, but as an inner ornamental pedal. Further, in Version 1, the entrance of the cello (m. *302*), which outlines root-position harmony, makes an emphatic articulation in the middle of the phrase, as opposed to the entrance of the cello on the third of the dominant chord in Version 2 (m. 285). Significantly, this occurs not in the middle of the phrase but only for the last measure; the cello entrance and its line impel the four-measure phrase to its close, and, at the same time, to the beginning of the next phrase. Perhaps the activity in the viola part (Version 1, mm. *302–3*) represents Beethoven's attempt to alleviate the lumpishness of the end of the first phrase. However, the result of the viola's action is just a false busyness of activity, a blurring rather than an increase of motion.

Whereas in Version 1 Beethoven adheres to a kind of block arrangement of the parts from phrase 1 (m. *300–303*) to phrase 2 (m. *304*), in Version 2 he energizes motion and mitigates the squareness of Version 1 by changing the arrangement of the concerting parts from the first phrase to the second. That is, the first and second violins lead in the first phrase, second violin and viola in the second. This in turn creates a registral continuity from the first violin in phrase 1 to the second violin in phrase 2 and contributes to the clear separation of the measure of "response" (m. 285) in the first violin.[158]

The revised disposition of the parts in Version 2 (the *galant* turn motive in the first violin, m. 282ff., is *above* rather than below the "countersubject") has another consequence: the turn motive (m. 284) follows, and forms part of, the linear descent of the *galant* figure, demonstrating their relationship, as it were. Although in retrospect the turn figure is more closely connected with the following triad in the first violin (m. 285), the linear continuity of measures 283–84 bonds this four-measure group. In Version 1, on the other hand, the turn figure is patently separated from both the *galant* figure and the "counter-

158. In Version 1, phrase 2 begins again in the viola with a marked disjunction in the main melodic line from the G of measures *302–3* in the first violin to low E and high C in the viola at measure *304*.

subject" reference. As a result, the relationship between the *galant* figure and the turn motive is less clear, and the coherence of the four-measure group is weaker.

Perhaps more importantly, the melodic and textural patterning established in measures 284–85 of Version 2 will ultimately relate both to that at measures 288–89 (the end of the next four-measure group) and to the succession of two-measure groups that form a six-measure unit from measure 288ff. This is not the case in Version 1, however, where the ends of the first two four-measure phrases do not "match." Thus, high-level phrase relationships are closely connected with the initial disposition of parts in each version.

The passage in measures *312–17*/294–99 (Ex. 41) leads toward the important penultimate cadence of the coda. In Version 1 this motion is considerably less cumulative than in Version 2. First, the internal division created by the occurrence of the turn motive in every measure in an outer voice (mm. *312–16*, first violin and cello) articulates each measure in Version 1. Second, the sforzando at the beginning of *each* measure emphasizes the measure-to-measure motion, as opposed to the placement of the sforzando every second measure in the analogous passage in Version 2 (mm. 294–98).

In Version 2 the direction and tension of the rising lines in the outer voices stand out at least partly because of the initial disposition of parts (Ex. 40, m. 282ff.). For, having set the quarter-note line, the "countersubject," *below* the *galant* treatment of the turn figure, Beethoven can keep the original turn motive (at mm. 284, 288, 290, 292) in the middle and low registers. He thereby avoids usurping the registral position of the six measures beginning at measure 294 (Ex. 41; cf. m. *312ff.*). As a result, these measures in Version 2 are clearly goal-directed in their ascent to the high D. In Version 1, by contrast, the steady rise (first violin) to measure *317* has far less power because the turn motive has already been heard three times (mm. *306, 308, 310*) in the very register to which the line rises. That is, the rise in measure *312ff.* is undermined by the immediately preceding position of the main line.

One of the striking revisions in the coda is that of the immediate approach to the penultimate F major cadence in Version 2.[159] For the very first time in the movement, the turn motive is used as a closing gesture: in measures 301–2 (Ex. 41) the motive on the fifth descends to the tonic. This moment is particularly touching—it is as if the motive, which has been so thoroughly worked, has simply given out. The effect of resignation in the three measures from measure 300 to 302 is understated. The treatment of these measures leaves room for a kind of coda to the coda, including a rollicking close at the very end. In contrast, the single chords on the first beats of measures *317–19* in Version 1 suggest greater finality, but at the same time they never bring the turn motive to rest as a closing gesture. The chordal effect is typically cadential in character but the special reinterpretation of the turn motive, which, after 300 measures (!), has been metamorphosed into a closing gesture, is simply missing in Version 1.[160]

Relationships over a distance: coda and development; coda and exposition.

The preceding discussion of texture and articulation leads to a consideration of the effects of the revisions on relationships over a musical distance: specifically, relationships between the passage at measure *300ff.*/282ff. in the coda and measure *137ff.*/129ff. in the development; between the passage beginning at measure *312*/294 (coda) and measure 13; and between the passage at measure *320ff.*/302ff. and those at measure 30ff. and *109ff.*/101ff.

159. In prospect, at least, this cadence may be heard as the main final cadence for the movement; then everything that follows may be heard as a peroration.

160. The conventional treatment of the turn motive as a closing gesture may be heard in Haydn's "Oxford" Symphony (No. 92), first movement, measures 74–75 and 197–98. The outline of the gesture, fifth to tonic, occurs frequently; see, for instance, Mozart's "Haffner" Symphony (No. 35), first movement, measures 73–74, and his "Linz" Symphony (No. 36), the very close of the trio of the third movement.

BEETHOVEN'S COMPOSITIONAL CHOICES

Example 40

In the passage at measure *300ff.*/282ff. (Ex. 40), the placement of the *galant* figure in the viola in Version 1, with the rising "countersubject" *above* it, not only creates a more ponderous movement than that in Version 2, but it only weakly suggests the resemblance of this passage to the fugato (Exx. 28 and 40). This is because the rising "countersubject" is a gesture that typically pushes *up* against a static or descending line, as in the fugato. Here, coming from above rather than below the main line, it is functionally atypical. By contrast, the revised placement of the *galant* figure in the first violin (mm. 282–83) and second violin (mm. 286–87) not only creates a sonorously lighter effect, but the relationship between the rising and descending lines is both more typical and more clearly a reference to the action of the fugato.[161]

In the passage between measures 294 and 299 in Version 2 (Ex. 41), the texture, articulation, and harmony (diminished seventh chords) are reminiscent of the motion at measure 13ff. (Ex. 1).[162] This reference is less audible in Version 1 (m. *312ff.*) because of the emphatic articulation of the turn motive in every measure. The allusion to the passage beginning at measure 13 in Version 2 is noteworthy for several reasons. First, it was this passage that led, in the exposition, to the first authentic cadence in the tonic (m. 20), a cadence that was also the penultimate close for the first key area. The passage between measures 294 and 299 leads, in analogous fashion, to the penultimate tonic close for the entire movement; the function of the coda passage is underlined by its association with that of the exposition. The reminiscence is perhaps especially appropriate because this passage was not included in the recapitulation; a digression (see pp. 75–78, and Ex. 37, m. *202ff.*/198ff.) replaced measures 9–29. Thus, the coda assumes some of the "responsibilities" of the recapitulation. Second, the rise to the high D (m. *317*/299) in the first violin (both versions) suggests the rise in the first violin line just before the emphatic cadence in F major at measure 29 in the exposition (see Exx. 1 and 40). But from his coordination of the treble and bass lines, it seems clear that in Version 2 Beethoven wants to emphasize the motion toward F; he takes the cello line up to C (m. 300) instead of stopping the linear ascent on B♭ as in Version 1 (m. *317*). (Also, as suggested above, the removal of two occurrences of the turn motive from Version 1 helps to focus attention on the linearity in Version 2.) Thus, although the allusion to measure 21ff. is present in both versions, the motion toward F is appropriately "raised to a higher power" in the coda of Version 2. The allusion to the motion toward the cadence at measure 29 also prepares us for what follows in the coda: a combined reminiscence of measure 30ff. and 105ff., as well as of the corresponding passage at the end of the recapitulation.[163]

Beethoven adds two measures to the phrase-group following the penultimate close (m. *320ff.*/302ff.), making this segment eight measures rather than six. This difference may be explained, at least partly, on two bases: (1) the eight-measure length (Version 2) corresponds to the same regular length of the analogous closing passage in both the exposition (Ex. 19, m. *109ff.*/101ff.) and recapitulation (no Ex., m. *280ff.*/262ff.); (2) more importantly, the two measures added in Version 2 (mm. 307–8) between the corresponding measures *324–25* in Version 1 underline the capsule reference (both versions) to the minor subdominant that figured prominently in the development (m. *157ff.*/151ff.) and in the "excursion" in the early part of the recapitulation.[164]

The added measures (mm. 307–8) also contribute to the melodic coherence of the

(See p. 94 for notes 161–164.)

Example 41

passage in Version 2. In Version 1 the repetition of the Bb–A (mm. *321–22*, first violin; mm. *323–24*, second violin) produces an additive pattern with virtually no momentum, and when the quarter-notes on A (m. *324*) move to Bb (m. *325*), a repetition of the preceding four-measure unit at the higher octave is suggested. This does not occur, and the result is a sense of incompleteness—even of abortion. In Version 2 there is considerably more motion because the line goes from Bb–A (mm. *305–6*) through Db–C (mm. *307–8*). Also, if the resolutions (mm. 306, 308) of appoggiaturas (mm. 305, 307) are heard as structural tones, then the triadic motion from F (m. 304) to A (m. 306) to C (m. 308) not only suggests continuation to the high F, but is related, by a kind of complementary inversion, to the descending triad (A–C–F) that follows in the last four measures of the movement. Moreover, the skip from C up to Bb (mm. 308–9) impels the line toward the A (m. 310) and the last four measures. In short, the patterning of Version 2 prepares for closure more strongly than does Version 1.

In both versions the last four measures of the movement are essentially the same.[165] And in both versions there is a contrast in character between the sudden vivacity of the final four measures and the quiescence of the immediately preceding passage (mm. *320–25/ 302–9*). In Version 2 the addition of the sforzandi on the third beats heighten this contrast[166] by intensifying motion across the bar-line; that is, the sforzando reinforces the action from one measure to the next instead of confining it within bar-lines.

161. This disposition of the parts is also more goal-directed in its implication of convergence of the two lines; contrastingly, the contrary motion outward in Version 1 does not imply convergence.

162. Ratner also suggests this in ''Key Definition,'' p. 476. He writes: ''the material associated with this cadence [m. 29] is withheld, only to return later, somewhat modified, to act as the final cadential point of arrival for the entire movement.''

163. The action in measures *320–26/302–10* alludes both to measure 30ff. in the exposition and to the close of both the exposition (m. *109ff./101ff.*) and recapitulation (m. *280ff./262ff.*). All three passages have in common the treatment of the turn motive as an ornamental pedal figure, as well as a melodic line with an anacrusis to an appoggiatura figure (cf. mm. *30–31ff.* and mm. *323–24/305–6*). The sixteenth-note figure in Example 41, measure *321ff./303ff.*, is heard in all of the closing passages.

164. I recognize the possibility that the ornamental sixteenth-note figure (as in m. *321ff./303ff.*) might be analyzed as a decoration of E (rather than F), in which case the harmony of the measure would be construed as dominant function over a tonic pedal, rather than as a minor subdominant ornamentation of the tonic.

165. In addition to the differences in dynamic markings, discussed in the text, there is a difference in bowing on the figure ♪♫ . One suspects that in Version 1 Beethoven was likening the figure to that near the beginning of the coda (m. *300ff./ 282ff.*), whereas in Version 2 the bowed articulation of the motive is like that of the original turn motive, the motive as it was first heard.

166. In Version 2 Beethoven also heightens local contrast by saving the crescendo for just the measure before the final four-measure group (as compared with the two-measure crescendo at m. *324* in Version 1); he even reiterates the dynamic marking of *pp* in measure 308, despite the fact that *pp* has been the prevailing dynamic from measure 300 on.

6

CONCLUDING REMARKS

THE SIMILARITY OF THE LAST FOUR MEASURES in both versions calls attention to the fact that decisive points in the form, such as the very beginning and the very end, are not fundamentally revised. Nor are the other moments that most basically delineate the large structure—the very beginnings of the development, recapitulation, and coda. Yet it seems clear that "to write quartets properly" meant more than merely to use the medium effectively. For even those considerable revisions that have most to do with the effective use of the medium (revisions involving scoring, part-writing, texture, and figuration, for example)—what we might assume Beethoven himself referred to in his letter to Amenda[167]—have been shown significantly to affect process and structure. Nevertheless, in reviewing the main types of revisions, it seems appropriate to group them into revisions related primarily to scoring, and revisions not necessarily occasioned by, or dependent on, scoring.

Revisions related primarily to scoring.

Frequently, revisions of texture create or heighten signs of formal function. To recall but a few: a rhythmic unison texture replaces an ongoing accompanimental pattern to signal the poise on V/V in the transition; revisions accommodate a gradual intensification of texture and sonority and a convergence of lines in a textural unison—a way of heralding the second key area and of making a smooth connection to the solo line that actually begins the second key area; the merging of lines at the end of the exposition serves as a way of drawing together and stabilizing all action at the end of the exposition. Elsewhere, and for opposite functions, revised instrumentation-cum-texture works just in reverse. For example, in the plateau, a flattening out of texture replaces a textural crescendo (that is, the continuous buildup in density of activity in Version 1 is leveled) to underline harmonic patterning, form, and expressive character.

That orchestration, in intimate connection with register and part-writing, was integral to Beethoven's sense of "how to write quartets properly" is apparent from numerous revisions. Just a few will be reviewed. Revised scoring not only enhances continuity and coherence in the first period of the second key area, but in one way or another contributes to

167. See p. 1.

---

the shaping of every cadence in the second key area. Combined with registral revisions, changes in instrumentation help to keep the high C of the first authentic cadence of the second key area (Exx. 12 and 14, m. 72) a focal tone and to enhance momentum beyond that cadence. Changes in instrumental doubling combine with registral revisions, first to strengthen the motion toward arrival at measure 84 (Ex. 15), and then, with an augmentation of texture, to intensify and dramatize the most formal cadence of the second key area (Ex. 17, m. 101). The latter revisions also create a linear continuity, absent in the corresponding passage of Version 1, as well as an internal coherence that bridges affective contrast within the period that closes at measure 101.

Revisions of instrumentation and register also figure importantly in the development and coda. Where registral problems in Version 1 produced confusion both before and during the fugato—by simultaneously setting up sham continuities and disrupting implicit ones—revisions of instrumentation, voice-leading, and register increase mobility and altogether clarify lines of action and local syntax (measure-groupings, for example). Where there was doubt about the integrity of formal units in the fugato of Version 1, registral disjunctions in Version 2 (registral analogs of deceptive cadences in harmony), made possible by revised instrumentation-cum-register, help to define implicit linear continuity and to delimit and integrate each segment. At the same time, modified part-writing intensifies instability within segments of the fugato (e.g., by heightening leading-tone drive in the C minor segment). In the first part of the retransition, the change in sonority to a reiteration of the rich middle-register sound of V_4^6 (second violin and viola; Ex. 34, mm. 167–71) underlines instability and emphasizes the need for resolution. In the coda, revised part-writing and instrumentation mitigate the squareness of Version 1, create clear registral continuities, and virtually demonstrate relationships between melodic figures in a way that is missing in Version 1. Revisions of instrumentation also affect high-level phrase relationships which are clarified within the coda as well as over the musical distance; that is, revisions of scoring make the coda's reference to the fugato much clearer in Version 2.

Revisions of figuration are, in part, closely allied with Beethoven's changed notions of how to write for four string instruments, of what is characteristic for strings as opposed to keyboard figuration. And, as with other changes of detail, such revisions often affect mobility and closure. This seems clear, for example, when one recalls the figuration in the first violin preceding the second key area (Ex. 10, mm. 49–55); Beethoven replaces the rather pianistic and closed figuration of Version 1 with a violinistic and more open-ended one. Similarly, in the plateau, along with the deletion of the miscast upbeat-figure, the accompanimental figuration—''flattened out'' to a two-note chord that is much more violinistic than the seesaw between pitches in Version 1 (e.g., second violin in Ex. 33, m. 157ff.)—promotes the understated and reined-in affect of the passage.

In general, Beethoven softens figuration by damping the degree of activity and making patterns less pronounced. Each such revision has consequences for larger-scale patterning. The more uniform figuration of the inner parts in the beginning of the transition affects conflicting measure-groupings and ultimately contributes to the resultant syntactic ambiguity—the preeminent aspect of the revised first part of the transition. The damping of the degree of activity in the inner parts in the closing area of the exposition (Ex. 19, m. 105ff.)

contributes to a weakening of pronounced regularity of frequent punctuation (every two measures) in Version 1 and fosters the greater stability of the closing area in Version 2. Newly created reciprocal relationships between similar patterning in the cello and first violin increase internal coherence. At the same time, perhaps paradoxically, the "leveling" of figuration in Version 2 also emphasizes certain aspects of process in the closing area.

As with figuration, the most typical revisions of dynamics include "leveling," the softening of contrasts, and the reduction in the frequency of dynamic emphases. Beethoven's revisions of dynamics are mainly deletions. For example, in the closing passage of the exposition, deletions of dynamics go hand in hand with the changes in figuration just referred to. Together, these help to eradicate the lumpish quality of movement. Sometimes, as with the deletions of sforzandi before the second authentic cadence of the second key area (Ex. 15, m. 84), dynamic understatement contributes to the heightening of anacrustic function. The revised placement of dynamics within segments of the fugato, for example, was shown to increase energy at the ends of those segments and to contribute to rhythmic integration.

The other principal type of change is the change in the reigning dynamic level (usually in conjunction with other aspects of overstatement) from *forte* to *piano*—as in the striking example of the last eight measures of the retransition where the *piano* helps to create a hushed containment. In the transition Beethoven rewrites a passage of undifferentiated *forte* to include a sudden *piano* that dramatizes arrival at V/V; this in turn allows for a crescendo that intensifies motion toward the second key area. Finally, dynamics are several times revised so that they function in a manner similar to the primary parameter of harmony. For instance, in the digression of the recapitulation, the crescendo to a *piano*, at precisely the point when the goal of motion is realized in other parameters, marks the moment in much the same way that a deceptive cadence functions harmonically (Ex. 35, m. 198); and the denial of the expected *forte* dynamic at the first emphatic cadence of the second key area (Ex. 11, m. 72) increases ongoing motion.

Revisions not primarily dependent on scoring.

Many of the most significant revisions of functions and large-scale structure may be viewed as more generally compositional, that is, not generated by or dependent on medium. In the broadest sense, there is the overall compression as evidenced in the removal of the double ending and repeat for the recapitulation and in the altogether shorter length of Version 2. Telescoping of two passages in particular shortens Version 2: eight measures excised after the first authentic cadence in the second key area (Ex. 14; also at its rhyme in the recapitulation) and six measures taken from the recalled transition that occurs in both versions in the recapitulation (Ex. 37). In the latter, telescoping not only shortens and tightens the line of action, but forges a completely new connection between the transitional segments of the exposition and recapitulation, thus fusing two thematic elements that were separated in the exposition.

A tightening of action manifests itself as well in virtually all the other revisions that one might class as not specifically generated by matters of scoring. These revisions create a structure whose important formal articulations or junctures are made more emphatic, while punctuations within periods are, on the whole, fewer or softened. In short, the reduction and lightening of intermediate closures tighten and enhance large-scale continuity. Two striking instances of markedly altered mobility may be recalled: motion into and through the fugato and action in the plateau.

Before the fugato, harmony is revised to prevent the B♭ from sounding like a tonic; instead, in Version 2 a twist of harmony makes B♭ sound like a deceptive cadence, linking this cadence at measure 129 with the one at measure 119 and thus revealing the quasi-parenthetical nature of the material between those measures (Ex. 22). As a result, D minor arrives as the long-range goal of the material on A that opened the development. In the same passage, other changes highlight the beginning of the fugato (at best an equivocal moment in Version 1): revisions of line and a clarification of phrase structure are effected by registral modifications, by deletions of the turn motive and its melodic prefiguring of the fugato in Version 1, and by the replacement of ambiguous silence by an echo.

In the plateau of Version 1, Beethoven's premature and powerful establishment of F minor by its dominant (C_2^4) severely undercuts the high-level motion into the retransition and especially into the recapitulation (Ex. 33, mm. *165ff.*). In Version 2 a markedly different harmonic organization, with F minor in a pivotal position rather than as a goal, makes the entire passage at once more processive and more clearly patterned. A revised tonal plan creates new relationships within the plateau and, more importantly, a much closer harmonic connection between the plateau and the subsequent dominant pedal passage. As mentioned earlier, the effect of the plateau in Version 1 is also spoiled by excess surface rhythmic activity (excess division), a result of the prominent upbeat figure and the other accompaniment figure, both of which detract from the swing of four-measure modules that Beethoven establishes as the basic units of structure in Version 2. Briefly, in this case Beethoven's understanding of the fundamental unit of action seems to have changed—or was it simply his understanding of how to project that unit of action?

Just as the revisions that occur before the fugato significantly affect the way we apprehend the beginning of the fugato itself, so the textural and figural revisions of the plateau exemplify changes that palpably affect both the internal structure of a given formal segment and its contiguous passages. For the removal of the upbeat figure from the plateau does not merely enhance affect and coherence within the plateau; significantly, it does not upstage its own later efficacy in animating the retransition.

At times simple revisions of melodic detail tighten high-level linear continuity through a musical period. One such instance (not particularly linked with scoring and idiomatic figuration for the medium) is the addition of the appoggiatura to the first violin part in the latter part of the transition (Ex. 4, mm. 43 and 45). This melodic change helps to focus attention on the harmonic process of the transition. What is of particular interest about the added appoggiaturas is that they mark the resumption of a sequential pattern that had been temporarily abandoned. This sequential pattern, which now spans intervening foreground events, intensifies the trajectory to the dominant of the dominant in preparation for the second key area.

Closely allied with revisions in the degree of local versus large-scale articulation are the many modifications that contribute to cumulative rather than additive measure-grouping and phrase structure—for instance, the more integrated phrase-grouping of the opening period of the second key area; the more closely welded six-measure segments in the fugato; and the more cumulative phrase patterning of the excursion early in the recapitulation. In most instances, one of the chief agents of the change from overly punctuated or additive construction to a longer-ranged, more cumulative motion, is the *removal* of melodic figures—for example, deletion of the turn motive before the fugato and deletion of the upbeat figure in the plateau. One change worthy of recall, however, involves *addition*: two added measures at the end of the fugato (Ex. 28) pave the way for the structural lengths of the plateau and smooth the connection into the next segment. Also contrary to what one might infer from the rubric "cumulative," Version 2 is sometimes more symmetrically shaped than Version 1. This is true of the plateau, where, in addition to the changed harmonic patterning, understatement allows for greater symmetry.

While all the revisions summarized up to now affect syntax, the realization of syntax may also be affected by changes that do not readily fall into categories already discussed. These revisions will now be reviewed. The more patent realization of syntax occurs on many levels of structure. On the most local levels there is such clarification of syntax as: the chord specification (Ex. 1, m. 5) that makes measure-groupings and phrase relationships clear, the removal of chord specification (Ex. 10, m. 55) that increases mobility into the second key area, or the changed disposition of a chord that intensifies local instability (for instance, the diminished seventh chord in the G minor segment of the fugato; Ex. 29).

The role of echoes in defining and clarifying phrase structure has been put into high relief by revisions in two different passages. Before the fugato Beethoven adds an echo that delimits a pattern, where there was only ambiguous silence in Version 1 (Ex. 22, m. *133*/125); that echo also helps to define measure-groupings within the entire passage. Locally it functions as a sign of the end of a phase of movement and as such makes immediately clear that the beginning of the fugato is indeed a beginning. Further, in terms of relationships over a distance, the echo acts as a sign that this passage will continue in a different manner than the earlier one (mm. 5–6, without echo) with which it could be associated; yet, at the same time, it suggests the relationship between the two passages.

Again, in the excursion early in the recapitulation, an echo (here involving the addition of two measures) clarifies local syntax by creating a statement-counterstatement relationship; it also makes clear that certain measures are parenthetical to the basic linear motion. In the same passage, harmonic goals are much clearer (in Version 1 arrival at G♭ major is weak; in Version 2 the entire passage of digression or excursion may be understood retrospectively in relation to G♭).

More broadly speaking, both anacrustic and stabilizing functions are heightened in numerous revisions. Anacrustic functions are strengthened throughout the motion into and through the first part of the second key area, and they are strikingly intensified in the retransition. Stabilizing functions are enhanced by revisions of the closing areas of the exposition and recapitulation, as well as by revision of the entire coda. One detail epitomizes such revisions: in the coda of Version 2 the turn motive is transformed into a closing gesture, an interpretation that never occurs in Version 1.

Part of the revision of high-level structure involves the more patent realization of thematic and harmonic relationships over a distance. Beethoven strengthens the following relationships: those between the exposition and development, by emphasizing parallelism in key relationships between the first part of the exposition and the development up through the fugato (see pp. 39 and 47–49); between the exposition and the coda, by heightening correspondences between measure 13ff. and measure 294ff. (see p. 92); and between the development (fugato segment) and the coda, by making textures more conventional and by demonstrating motivic similarities and connections (see pp. 88, 92). Such relationships over a distance contribute to the intensification of large-scale coherence.

The more patent realization of high-level structure is also a function of radical revisions of the harmonic plan. The most striking instances of this are, of course, in the fugato and the plateau. In the fugato, the succession of tonal centers in Version 2 is D minor, G minor, C minor, F minor, B♭ minor, as compared with those in Version 1: G minor, C minor, F minor, B♭ minor. Similarly, in the plateau (whose harmonic plan considerably affects subsequent events), the harmonic plans vary significantly: B♭ minor, G♭ major, C as dominant, F minor in Version 1, as compared with B♭ minor, G♭ major, F minor, D♭ major in Version 2.

Some of the similarities in kinds of revisions suggest that Beethoven viewed certain passages as comparable. Recall, for instance, the similarities among revisions at the beginning of the transition, those following the first authentic cadence in the second key area, and those in the final part of the closing area of the exposition. Paradoxically, the similarity in the nature of the revisions calls attention to differences in function (see p. 35).

Changes from exposition to recapitulation *within* Version 1 appear to have influenced Beethoven's revision of both exposition and recapitulation in Version 2. His working out of the recapitulation in Version 1 seems to have suggested alternatives to some of the compositional problems of the exposition, but he did not go back to correct himself in the exposition of Version 1. These new solutions were then carried over to the exposition of Version 2 and, quite naturally, into the recapitulation of Version 2 as well. For example, a gradual recognition of possible relationships between materials from two previously separate segments of the transition seems indicated by the revisions of the G♭ major segment of the recapitulation (see p. 79). In the exposition of Version 2, Beethoven incorporates changes he had *begun* to make as early as the writing out of the recapitulation in Version 1 (as compared with the exposition of the corresponding passage). In other words, for a few passages Beethoven really began revisions in the recapitulation of Version 1. As a result, there is a kind of progress from exposition to recapitulation in Version 1 to exposition and recapitulation in Version 2. Whereas these changes occurred in stages in the case of the transition, Beethoven's revisions of the second key area in the recapitulation of Version 1 are carried over intact to both the exposition and recapitulation of Version 2.

Despite the generalizations I have made about Beethoven's revisions in the first movement of Op. 18, No. 1, it should be clear that such generalization is *not* what is specially interesting. What is interesting, it seems to me, are the particulars, about which one cannot readily generalize. For there is scarcely a revision that does not involve the intricate connection of several parameters—at once, in prospect, in retrospect, or in some combination of these.

Common musicological sense and some acquaintance with Beethoven's workshop, via sketch and autograph studies, would suggest the general types and nature of revisions—for example, smoother connections; greater focus; less stock or conventional figuration; refinements of part-writing, figuration, phrase structure, and scoring; even clarification of large-scale structure.[168] *That* Beethoven alters these is predictable. *How* he does so, and *why*, is surely less so. And it is the how and why that have been my principal concerns. To this end I have almost constantly, although mostly tacitly, invoked theory—sometimes established theories, at other times nascent theories of my own—about such fundamental matters as the nature of coherence in musical relationships, the creation of articulation, anacrustic versus non-anacrustic functions, additive versus cumulative structure; and about such less fundamental matters as the way echoes may work or the quasi-syntactic use of texture. Although the purpose of my study has not been the explicit formulation of general principles, I would, nevertheless, like to think that a number of its specific points have implications for music theory.

Whatever the implications for theory may prove to be, my main and persistent concern has been to account for the nature of Beethoven's compositional choices as they can be understood from a comparison of the two versions of the first movement of his String Quartet Op. 18, No. 1. I hope that I have shown how Beethoven's revisions not only set character and syntax in high relief but significantly affect both the large-scale process and the formal integrity of the entire movement, and how even the most modest changes are, in a fundamental sense, compositional.

168. Those who would have liked a typology of Beethoven's revisions and/or a history of his style of revising are bound to be disappointed by the limited generalizations I have made. But because serious analytic-critical study—as opposed to description—of Beethoven's compositional choices is still in its infancy, there is as yet no solid basis for more extensive generalization. That is, with few other studies to connect with mine (particularly studies of two versions of one work, close in time), further generalization about the typicality of the revisions in Op. 18, No. 1 would, I think, be premature. I hope, however, that my study may eventually contribute to both a typology and a history of Beethoven's style of revising.